# DISEASES AND DISORDERS

# PHOBIAS
## WHEN FEAR BECOMES IRRATIONAL

By Maeve Losito

Portions of this book originally appeared in *Phobias* by Jenny MacKay.

LUCENT PRESS

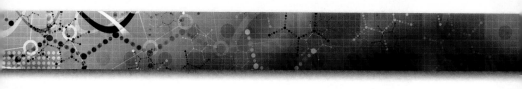

Published in 2020 by
**Lucent Press, an Imprint of Greenhaven Publishing, LLC**
353 3rd Avenue
Suite 255
New York, NY 10010

Designer: Deanna Paternostro
Editor: Jennifer Lombardo

**Library of Congress Cataloging-in-Publication Data**

Names: Losito, Maeve, author.
Title: Phobias : when fear becomes irrational / Maeve Losito.
Description: New York : Lucent Press, [2020] | Series: Diseases and disorders
  | Includes bibliographical references and index.
Identifiers: LCCN 2018050509 (print) | LCCN 2018051942 (ebook) | ISBN
  9781534567467 (eBook) | ISBN 9781534567450 (pbk. book : alk. paper) | ISBN
  9781534566941 (library bound book : alk. paper)
Subjects: LCSH: Phobias. | Phobias–Treatment.
Classification: LCC RC535 (ebook) | LCC RC535 .L67 2020 (print) | DDC
  616.85/225–dc23
LC record available at https://lccn.loc.gov/2018050509

Printed in the United States of America

CPSIA compliance information: Batch #BS19KL: For further information contact Greenhaven Publishing LLC, New York,
New York, at 1-844-317-7404.

Please visit our website, www.greenhavenpublishing.com. For a free color catalog of all our
high-quality books, call toll free 1-844-317-7404 or fax 1-844-317-7405.

# CONTENTS

Illness is an unfortunate part of life, and it is one that is often misunderstood. Thanks to advances in science and technology, people have been aware for many years that diseases such as the flu, pneumonia, and chickenpox are caused by viruses and bacteria. These diseases all cause physical symptoms that people can see and understand, and many people have dealt with these diseases themselves. However, sometimes diseases that were previously unknown in most of the world turn into epidemics and spread across the globe. Without an awareness of the method by which these diseases are spread—through the air, through human waste or fluids, through sexual contact, or by some other method—people cannot take the proper precautions to prevent further contamination. Panic often accompanies epidemics as a result of this lack of knowledge.

Knowledge is power in the case of mental disorders, as well. Mental disorders are just as common as physical disorders, but due to a lack of awareness among the general public, they are often stigmatized. Scientists have studied them for years and have found that they are generally caused by chemical imbalances in the brain, but they have not yet determined with certainty what causes those imbalances or how to fix them. Because even mild mental illness is stigmatized in Western society, many people prefer not to talk about it.

Chronic pain disorders are also not well understood—even by researchers—and do not yet have foolproof treatments. People who have a mental disorder or a disease or disorder that causes them to feel chronic pain can be the target of uninformed

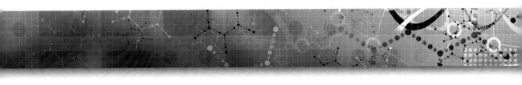

opinions. People who do not have these disorders sometimes struggle to understand how difficult it can be to deal with the symptoms. These disorders are often termed "invisible illnesses" because no one can see the symptoms; this leads many people to doubt that they exist or are serious problems. Additionally, people who have an undiagnosed disorder may understand that they are experiencing the world in a different way than their peers, but they have no one to turn to for answers.

Misinformation about all kinds of ailments is often spread through personal anecdotes, social media, and even news sources. This series aims to present accurate information about both physical and mental conditions so young adults will have a better understanding of them. Each volume discusses the symptoms of a particular disease or disorder, ways it is currently being treated, and the research that is being done to understand it further. Advice for people who may be suffering from a disorder is included, as well as information for their loved ones about how best to support them.

With fully cited quotes, a list of recommended books and websites for further research, and informational charts, this series provides young adults with a factual introduction to common illnesses. By learning more about these ailments, they will be better able to prevent the spread of contagious diseases, show compassion to people who are dealing with invisible illnesses, and take charge of their own health.

# IRRATIONAL FEARS

In many societies, fear is not considered a valid emotion. People who give in to fear may be made fun of by others who do not understand it, and worrying that this will happen can add to a person's fears and keep them from telling someone who might help them. Many people are told to face their fears so they can conquer them, and while this may be helpful for some, it is not an easy thing for someone with a mental illness to do on their own.

Most people are unaware that fear is actually a widespread mental health problem. Millions of people do not have the ability to calm themselves down when they encounter an object or situation that they find frightening. When someone's fear of something becomes so extreme that it interferes with the way they live their life, it is considered a type of mental illness called a phobia. For some people, even the thought of their phobia is enough to cause a panic attack.

The term "phobia" comes from the ancient Greeks. The Greeks believed that senseless fears were the mischievous work of Phobos, the god of fright. The Greeks also believed that the god of nature, Pan, put fear into those who were close enough to him to hear his angered voice, which is where the modern word "panic" comes from.

One of the first documented cases of a patient with a phobia dates back at least 2,400 years to

Shown here is a representation of Phobos, the Greek god of fear.

Hippocrates, an ancient Greek physician who wrote about Damocles, a man who was afraid of heights. Hippocrates also documented another man who was struck by horror at the sound of a flute playing after dark. The ancient Greeks had no explanation for what could make an otherwise sensible man tremble at the sight or sound of something that posed little or no danger. The only explanation that appeared logical was the involvement of their gods. Today, although supernatural causes have been ruled out, the question of what, exactly, causes phobias is still under investigation.

In the 1800s, doctors and scientists began creating an extensive list of potential causes of phobias. Others, however, did not bother to understand their fearful patients and simply dulled the panic attacks with a powerful drug called opium. This drug caused more problems than it solved by creating an addiction in people who took it. The medical causes behind panic attacks and the phobias that trigger them remain a mystery, but research has gotten medical experts closer to the answer than they were in past decades. One of the things doctors do know about phobias is that they are common. There is also evidence to support the theory that phobias are learned behaviors, since children who have a parent with a phobia often grow up to suffer from phobias themselves. Other research supports the idea that phobias are at least partially genetic, or passed down from parent to child, as there have been studies conducted on identical twins who were separated at birth but reported having the same phobia. Certain types of phobias are more common among particular age groups than others—for example, young children are more likely to be afraid of the dark than adults—but others can affect anyone, and it is difficult to predict who will develop a phobia or what the object of the phobia will be.

Some people enjoy feeling temporarily frightened, which is why haunted houses are popular around Halloween. However, phobic reactions are far worse than the normal fear response people experience while riding a roller coaster or watching a scary movie. Encountering a phobia trigger can provoke a panic attack, causing the person to experience symptoms such as light-headedness, nausea, sweating, difficulty breathing, heart palpitations, and derealization (a feeling of being disconnected from reality). In some cases, the symptoms are so strong that the person feels as though they are dying. Although they are not actually dying, the experience is frightening and feels real to the individual experiencing it in that moment.

People who have a phobia generally realize that their fear is illogical, but that knowledge does not give them control over it. Unlike someone who goes to a haunted house and is only moderately frightened because they know the things they are seeing cannot hurt them, someone with a phobia can look at something with the knowledge that it will not hurt them yet still be unable to control their panic. This lack of control can lead them to develop behaviors to avoid their phobia trigger so they do not have to experience a panic attack at all. However, depending on how

Some people enjoy fear-themed attractions such as this one.

frequently their phobia is encountered in daily life, these behaviors can keep them from traveling, going to college, dating, or having their dream job. In this way, phobias can truly ruin lives.

Because avoiding phobia triggers can be difficult—and in some cases, even impossible—many people end up having to figure out a way to overcome their fear. This is not as simple as it sounds, though; it is generally a long and stressful process that involves therapy and sometimes prescription medication. Modern technology can help by giving people a safe way to confront certain phobias, such as heights or driving, through computer-simulated experiences.

There is no single, quick cure for a phobia; overcoming one takes dedication and time. However, with the help of experts and loved ones, it is possible for someone with a phobia to live a normal, happy life.

# CHAPTER ONE

# UNDERSTANDING PHOBIAS

Phobias are classified by the medical community as a type of anxiety disorder. Other anxiety disorders include generalized anxiety disorder (GAD), post-traumatic stress disorder (PTSD), social anxiety disorder (SAD), agoraphobia, and obsessive-compulsive disorder (OCD). However, out of all of these, phobias are the most common. According to the Anxiety and Depression Association of America (ADAA), about 8.7 percent of American adults have at least one phobia, and many have more than one.

There are many potentially harmful and deadly things in the world, and fear of these things is a natural instinct that animals and people experience as a means of survival. For example, people who are nervous around snakes and avoid them when they find them in the wild are less likely to be bitten by a venomous one. Having a certain amount of fear of potentially dangerous things is normal and natural. In normal circumstances, this fear does not arise unless the person is directly confronted with the object or situation.

However, human fears do not always serve a survival purpose. It is one thing to be scared of something that is actually dangerous, such as falling off a cliff or getting buried in an avalanche, but it is another matter when people fear things that cannot harm or kill them, or that they are unlikely to encounter in their everyday life. For example, being afraid of bears is natural, but for someone who lives in the city and panics when they see a bear on television or in a book, this fear is not useful. When a fear becomes so extreme that it interferes with a person's life for at least six months, it can be classified as a phobia.

The cobra is an easily recognizable venomous snake. Even people who normally like seeing these snakes at a zoo may be scared if they see one in the wild. This is a case when fear is a helpful survival tool.

## The Impact on Quality of Life

People who have phobias are so frightened of the situation or object that scares them that they will do almost anything to avoid it. Phobias force people to make choices they might not make if it were not for their fear.

According to the fifth edition of the *Diagnostic and Statistical Manual of Mental Disorders* (*DSM-5*), the book experts use to diagnose mental illnesses, "Fear is the emotional response to real or perceived imminent threat, whereas anxiety is anticipation of future threat."[1] For example, someone who has a fear of spiders may not want to get close to one for fear that it will crawl on them or bite them, while someone with a phobia may not even want to look at a picture of a spider. The person with a phobia is reacting to the idea that they might be in danger from a spider in the future.

Phobias vary in severity, so not everyone reacts the same way to their phobia trigger. One person with a phobia of spiders may panic at the sight of even a photo of a spider but behave normally as long as they cannot see the object of their fear. Another may be so preoccupied with their fear that they check their bed for spiders every night before they go to sleep and refuse to wear open-toed shoes outside in case a spider crawls on their foot.

The quality of life for someone with a severe phobia deteriorates further when their fear affects their social life. For example, someone with a fear of dogs will likely refuse to visit the house of a friend who

People with leporiphobia are scared of rabbits, even though they are rarely aggressive. Some people whose leporiphobia is less severe may be able to handle looking at or being around rabbits in certain circumstances.

has a dog or be around the friend if there is a chance the dog will be there as well. They may also refuse to go anywhere a dog is likely to be, and since people generally walk their dogs on public sidewalks, this can greatly restrict where the person with the phobia is willing to walk. People who have phobias are essentially habitual avoiders. Some avoid specific things or situations that scare them, while others try to avoid even the thought of their trigger.

Mental health experts can determine the severity of a phobia by giving their patients a questionnaire that was created by the American Psychiatric Association (APA). From a scale of zero, or "never," to four, or "all of the time," the patient ranks how frequently in the past week they have experienced phobia symptoms in specific situations, such as driving, flying, being around insects or needles, or encountering water. These include things such as "felt moments of sudden terror, fear, or fright in these situations," "felt tense muscles, felt on edge or restless, or had trouble relaxing in these situations," and "distracted myself to avoid thinking about these situations."[2] There are 10 questions in total, and the higher the final score, the more severe the phobia is. Some people have a phobia so mild and so infrequently encountered that they do not need treatment; for example, someone with a phobia of flying who does not have to travel frequently—and can choose to drive instead when they do—would probably not seek treatment. On the other hand, someone with a phobia of flying who is required to take an airplane for frequent business trips would likely benefit from treatment.

## Categorizing Phobias

Specific phobias are broken down into categories based on the trigger. Animal phobia is the fear of

## How Much Would You Pay?

Richard I. Garber, who runs a blog about public speaking, gave an example to help people understand the difference between a fear and a phobia:

> One simple way to think about the difference is just to ask how much money you would be willing to pay to avoid giving a speech. Would it be:
>
> A. $0.10
> B. $100
> C. $100,000
> D. $100,000,000
> E. $100,000,000,000
>
> If you answered A or B, then you just have a fear. If you answered E … then you definitely have a phobia.[1]

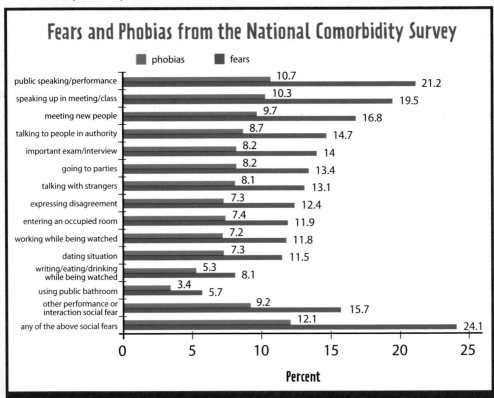

### Fears and Phobias from the National Comorbidity Survey

■ phobias   ■ fears

| | phobias | fears |
|---|---|---|
| public speaking/performance | 10.7 | 21.2 |
| speaking up in meeting/class | 10.3 | 19.5 |
| meeting new people | 9.7 | 16.8 |
| talking to people in authority | 8.7 | 14.7 |
| important exam/interview | 8.2 | 14 |
| going to parties | 8.2 | 13.4 |
| talking with strangers | 8.1 | 13.1 |
| expressing disagreement | 7.3 | 12.4 |
| entering an occupied room | 7.4 | 11.9 |
| working while being watched | 7.2 | 11.8 |
| dating situation | 7.3 | 11.5 |
| writing/eating/drinking while being watched | 5.3 | 8.1 |
| using public bathroom | 3.4 | 5.7 |
| other performance or interaction social fear | 9.2 | 15.7 |
| any of the above social fears | 12.1 | 24.1 |

Percent

It is common for people to be nervous or uncomfortable in certain social situations, but phobias are less common, as this information from the 2008 National Comorbidity Survey Replication shows.

1. Richard I. Garber, "What's the Difference Between a Fear and a Phobia?," *Joyful Public Speaking (from Fear to Joy)*, October 11, 2011. joyfulpublicspeaking.blogspot.com/2011/10/whats-difference-between-fear-and.html.

animals or insects. Natural environment phobias involve a fear of storms, heights, darkness, or water. People who have an abnormal fear of blood, getting injections, or being injured suffer from blood-injection-injury type phobia. Situational type phobias can be triggered by different types of transportation, such as cars, airplanes, and buses, or enclosed places such as tunnels or elevators. There is also an "other" category that covers phobias that are not easily categorized, such as a fear of loud noises, clowns, or vomiting.

Some people develop phobias after being exposed to something that scares them. For example, in the *Harry Potter* series, Ron Weasley is afraid of spiders because when he was three years old, his brother turned his teddy bear into a spider while he was holding it. Other people cannot point to a specific incident that caused their phobia. This may be because there was none or because they cannot remember it.

Animal phobias are among the most common in the world; the top 13 most common phobias that were reported in a British government survey included ophidiophobia (fear of snakes), arachnophobia (fear of spiders), musophobia (fear of mice), and cynophobia (fear of dogs). These phobias make sense when it comes to helping the species survive: Some spiders and snakes are venomous, and being afraid of them would minimize the chances of being bitten; dogs that are not well trained, such as ones a person might encounter in the wild, can be vicious; and living in close quarters with mice can transmit diseases that are fatal to humans. Other, less common animal phobias are less clearly connected to a survival instinct. These include ichthyophobia (fear of fish), helminthophobia (fear of worms), and zoophobia (fear of all animals).

Natural environment phobias are also very

common. In a British government survey, acrophobia (fear of heights) was reported as the most common fear, with nearly 58 percent of respondents saying they were affected—23 percent of whom said they were very afraid, and 35 percent of whom said they were only a little afraid. British novelist Patrick McGrath said his fear of heights has kept him from doing certain things, such as hiking up mountains, for most of his life. A traumatic childhood event contributed to McGrath's acrophobia: He fell out of a tree and sustained a serious injury and a concussion. Since then, he said, his fear has "become stronger and stronger, to the point where I can't watch rooftop scenes in movies."[3] McGrath said he once suffered an attack of vertigo—a dizzy feeling that often accompanies acrophobia—during a drive through the mountains with his wife and stepson:

> I realized to my horror that the road had turned into a narrow gravel track and was climbing steeply with no barrier rail up the sheer cliff-face ... After about ten yards I was

The Angel's Landing trail at Zion National Park in Utah is very narrow with steep drop-offs. A chain is bolted to the cliff wall to help hikers keep their balance. Someone with a phobia of heights would avoid this trail.

*dripping with sweat, my knuckles were white, and I had to face the fact that I was terrified and couldn't go forward … I just had to reverse down onto safe ground.*[4]

Along with heights, fears of weather events fall into the category of natural environment phobias. Some of these are relatively easy to avoid, depending on where the person lives. For example, "the region from central Texas, northward to northern Iowa, and from central Kansas and Nebraska east to Western Ohio is often collectively known as 'Tornado Alley'"[5] because these are the areas in the United States where tornadoes are common. In contrast, someone with lilapsophobia (fear of tornadoes) who lives in New England, Alaska, or Hawai'i will almost never have to face their fear. However, even if they live in one of these places, someone whose

The fear of natural phenomena is not uncommon, even among those who are rarely or never exposed to particular weather patterns.

lilapsophobia is very severe may worry excessively about someday experiencing a tornado. This can cause unnecessary panic any time there is an average storm and can also prevent them from traveling to anywhere where tornadoes are more common. Psychologist John Westefeld has studied individuals with astraphobia (fear of thunder and lightning— not to be confused with astrophobia, or fear of outer space) and lilapsophobia, which are related phobias. In an article for *USA Today*, he said that there are some people "who are so debilitated by the thought of severe weather that they can't drive their cars or go to work or school."[6] These people are also likely to have panic attacks before or during a storm, including symptoms such as trembling, chest pain, difficulty breathing, and uncontrollable crying.

Thunderstorms, tornadoes, earthquakes, and other natural events sometimes happen with little or no warning. Therefore, people with specific phobias of natural phenomena may feel they have very little control over their fear. They cannot prevent a thunderstorm or predict when an earthquake might happen, so there is no guarantee that they can avoid it. They may feel a need to obsessively check weather reports or the safety of their home. Someone with severe astraphobia may choose not to leave their house on a day when the weather report calls for rain. However, since weather reports can be wrong, they may end up missing out on work, school, or social activities for no reason if the weather clears up unexpectedly. People without a weather-related phobia behave differently. Healthline explained,

*In people without this phobia, news of an impending storm may lead you to cancel or relocate outdoor plans. Or if you find yourself in a lightning storm, you may seek shelter or move away from tall trees. Even though the chances*

*of getting hit by lightning are slim, these actions represent an appropriate response to a potentially dangerous situation.*[7]

A third category of phobia is blood-injection-injury, in which people fear things such as getting sick, getting hurt, going to a doctor, seeing blood—either their own or others'—or getting injections. For example, someone with a severe case of mysophobia (fear of germs) could struggle with touching any surfaces for fear of the germs lurking on the surface. Mysophobia can create problems: Handling money, opening doors, answering telephones, and shaking people's hands are terrible experiences for someone with this phobia. They are so worried about getting sick that it becomes difficult to interact with people and do everyday activities.

Other people with illness-related phobias fear going to the doctor. Some people fear medical professionals themselves (latrophobia), which can prevent them from taking care of their health problems. Others only fear needles and getting injections (trypanophobia). Most people do not enjoy these things and may put off making an appointment longer than they should, but a phobia can cause severe health neglect. For example, people with severe dentophobia (fear of dentists) "will literally let their teeth rot out because they are afraid to go to a dentist,"[8] according to psychologist Sheryl Jackson.

The fear of a situation can be more troublesome than the fear of an object. For instance, people who are terrified of sheep can generally avoid them in day-to-day living as long as they do not live on or near a farm. However, people with a fear of crowded or small spaces such as elevators, stairwells, or subway trains tend to have a harder time, especially if they live in a city. This fear, called claustrophobia, is very common. It may take someone a long time to get somewhere, as they tend to go out of their way to avoid their trigger. Other common situational phobias include aviophobia (fear of flying), glossophobia (fear of public speaking), and enochlophobia (fear of crowds). Sometimes these are easily avoided, but other times they are necessary to face. Some uncommon phobias include taphophobia (fear of being buried alive), urophobia (fear of urinating), somniphobia (fear of falling asleep), and athazagoraphobia (fear of forgetting or being forgotten).

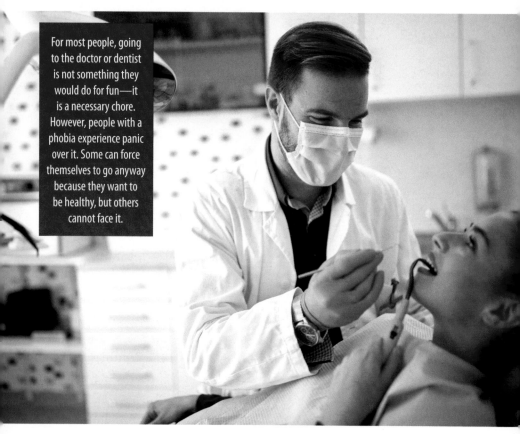

For most people, going to the doctor or dentist is not something they would do for fun—it is a necessary chore. However, people with a phobia experience panic over it. Some can force themselves to go anyway because they want to be healthy, but others cannot face it.

The "other" category of phobias is a catchall for anything that cannot be easily identified. For example, coulrophobia (fear of clowns) is very common, but as clowns are not an animal, a natural phenomenon, an illness, or a situation, there is no good specific category to put them in. The lines between the categories can sometimes be blurry; for example, some people might consider an encounter with a clown to be a situational fear, while others might put fear of a clown itself in the "other" category. However, categorization is not as important as diagnosis.

# Diagnosing Phobias

Several criteria must be present in order to diagnose a person with a specific phobia. These include:

- *Marked fear or anxiety about a specific object or situation.*

- *The phobic object or situation almost always provokes immediate fear or anxiety.*

- *The phobic object or situation is actively avoided or endured with intense fear or anxiety.*

- *The fear or anxiety is out of proportion to the actual danger posed by the specific object or situation and to the sociocultural context.*

- *The fear, anxiety or avoidance is persistent, typically lasting for six months or more.*

- *The fear, anxiety or avoidance causes clinically significant distress or impairment in social, occupational or other important areas of functioning.*

- *The disturbance is not better explained by the symptoms of another mental disorder.*[1]

The lines between mental disorders can get confusingly blurry sometimes, so careful questioning is required to make a diagnosis. For example, if the thought of going to the doctor makes someone panic or if they burst into tears while receiving an injection, they likely have a phobia of doctors or needles. In contrast, if they are afraid of saying or doing something embarrassing in front of their doctor, it is likely that they have social anxiety disorder rather than a specific phobia.

1. "Classifying Anxiety: Understanding the Difference Between Fear and Phobia," Grace College Online, accessed on October 3, 2018. online.grace.edu/news/human-services/difference-between-fear-and-phobia/.

## Social Anxiety versus Social Phobias

The fear of an object or situation is officially known as a specific phobia, although it is almost always simply called a phobia. Social anxiety disorder—a condition in which people are unnecessarily nervous and self-conscious in public places or situations—is not a specific phobia. However, someone may have one or more specific social phobias; they are fine with all social situations except those particular ones. Social phobias include fears such as speaking in public, talking on the phone, or interacting with cashiers. Many people are nervous in these situations and would prefer not to do things such as give a speech or have someone watch them eat, but people with a phobia get upset at the thought and panic when they encounter that situation.

Social anxiety disorder is sometimes known as social phobia, but it is not the same as a specific phobia. The Social Anxiety Institute has campaigned for more than 15 years to get people to stop using the term "social phobia." It listed several important reasons why "social anxiety" is a more accurate term, including:

1. *Most people, even professional organizations, have a difficult time understanding the definition of "social phobia." For example, the largest anxiety association in the world many times misuses the term. When it tries to give a case study or tell a story about a person with "social phobia," the story invariably turns into a story about a person with agoraphobia, an entirely different anxiety disorder.*

2. *The people, organizations, and sites that lump "the phobias" together are doing a real disservice not only to this problem ... but to the "true" phobias, such as specific phobias ... When an organization or group lists social anxiety as*

*part of "the phobias" it is a strong clue that they probably do not understand social anxiety, its complications, and its distinctiveness from other anxiety disorders.*[9]

## Agoraphobia

Agoraphobia is typically mischaracterized in the media as a simple fear of leaving the house. In reality, it is a more complex disorder with two variations. Because of these two distinct types, the *DSM-5* reclassified agoraphobia as its own separate disorder. People who have the more common type, agoraphobia with panic disorder, avoid places where they have already had a panic attack; for instance, if someone has a panic attack while they are grocery shopping, they may begin to order their groceries online to avoid going to a grocery store again. They also tend to avoid places where they cannot leave immediately if they start to have a panic attack, such as a sporting event. In severe cases, this can restrict the places they feel comfortable to just their own house, which is where the "fear of leaving the house" idea comes from.

Panic disorder is an anxiety disorder in which someone has unexplained, unpredictable panic attacks. In many cases, these are unconnected to whatever is happening around them, which makes them particularly troubling. Panic disorder affects about 3 percent of Americans, and around one in three of them develop agoraphobia as a result. This happens because the unpredictability of when and where a panic attack will strike makes people look for a way to address their feelings of being out of control. Restricting their travel only to places where they feel safe helps them feel they are in control again.

People who have the less common type of

agoraphobia, which is agoraphobia without panic disorder, typically avoid places because they have certain specific phobias, such as fear of experiencing a crime or terrorist attack or fear of getting a contagious disease from someone they encounter in a public space. If they have multiple phobias or ones they are likely to encounter frequently, this can make it difficult for them to find places where they feel safe.

Many people enjoy going to concerts, but for someone with agoraphobia, they can be stressful because it is hard to leave one quickly.

Phobias can have a huge negative effect on a person's daily life as well as their self-esteem. Most people with phobias are aware that their fears are irrational, but since a phobia is a mental illness, knowing this does nothing to stop the panic. They may be embarrassed to tell anyone about their phobia, especially if it is one of the less common ones. However, this prolongs the amount of time they spend panicking and avoiding objects or situations. If someone's phobias are causing them distress, seeking help from a mental health expert is important. Therapists are trained to work with many unusual illnesses and have studied how the brain works; they know that a person's mental illness is not their fault, and they do not judge their patients.

# CHAPTER TWO

# RISK FACTORS

Although researchers are still unsure of the exact causes of phobias, they do know that there are certain factors that make someone more likely to develop one. These risk factors are sometimes phobia-specific. For example, for some phobias, simply being a child is a risk factor. Astraphobia and nyctophobia (fear of the dark) are common childhood phobias. Most children outgrow them, but some carry these phobias into their adult years. Childhood phobias may be dismissed by parents as being normal, but studies have shown that this is not always the case. According to one study, about 2.3 percent of children in a sample community—a community where anxiety disorders among children were studied and observed—suffered from phobic symptoms extreme enough to qualify as clinical phobic disorder. In short, many children are occasionally fearful, but if these fears trouble a child on a regular basis or appear to become more extreme, parents should consider seeking medical help.

For certain other phobias, gender is a risk factor, as more women than men develop animal phobias and more men than women develop phobias of medical experts such as doctors and dentists. Women are also more likely than men to have any type of anxiety disorder. Some researchers believe this is because of differences in brain chemistry; for example, the hormones estrogen and progesterone, which are found in higher levels in women than in men, have been linked to increased activity in the parts of the brain that activate the fight-or-flight response.

People who suffer from phobias may be made fun of or fear being made fun of, especially if their trigger is something that is not typically dangerous, such as flowers or dust. However, phobias are no laughing matter, and having one does not make someone crazy. A phobia is a mental illness, which can sometimes be caused or made worse by another mental illness or disorder. For example, many people with autism have difficulty processing certain sensory stimulation, such as flashing lights or loud sounds. This can contribute to the development of astraphobia. People who have other anxiety disorders, such as GAD, are also more likely to develop a specific phobia.

## Who Develops Phobias?

Although mental health organizations have statistics on the number of people with phobias, these statistics do not include people who are undiagnosed or have not admitted to having a phobia. Helen Saul, author of *Phobias: Fighting the Fear*, wrote that the percentage might be even higher if more people were honest about their fears. Gender expectations are one of the things that can contribute to these skewed results. Women have "consistently higher fear ratings than men," according to Saul, but this is "possibly because men are less willing to admit to fears."[10] In Western society, men are generally expected to be brave, while women are more often seen as nervous and fearful. For this reason, it is considered more reasonable for a woman to have an irrational fear than a man. More research must be done to prove whether the gender imbalance is due to brain chemistry, socialization, or a combination of the two.

People of color also tend to be underrepresented in statistics. A 2015 study by the Substance Abuse and Mental Health Services Administration (SAMHSA) found that white adults, adults of two or more races, and Native Americans were the most likely to report seeking therapy or using medication to control their disorder. Black, Hispanic, and Asian adults were the least likely to do so. The study found that the high expense of services and participants' lack of insurance were the most common reasons why someone would not seek help. This problem is not easily fixed, as problems with the health insurance industry and racism against black and Latinx people that contributes to higher rates of poverty than the general population are two important issues that need to be addressed. This will require a drastic change in the way American society currently functions.

The idea of a monster in the closet is such a universal childhood fear that it was the subject of the 2001 movie *Monsters, Inc.* Many people eventually outgrow this fear.

Although a phobia can start at any age, some take root in childhood. Fears of weather, natural disasters, or animals are most likely to start when a person is young, and other phobias tend to develop if someone has a scary experience when they are young. For example, someone who was badly hurt by a dog when they were young is at a higher risk of developing cynophobia than someone who has only had positive encounters with dogs. In some cases, "a phobia can start with a small concern, which grows into a worry and then builds to become a full-blown phobia,"[11] journalist Madeleine Brindley wrote. For example, someone whose friend was bitten by a dog may worry that this will also happen to them one day.

Teenagers and adults can develop phobias too—even of things that never bothered them as kids. These fears are especially puzzling to the medical community because they seem to come out of nowhere. A 30-year-old who thought nothing of heights as a young kid might suddenly start to sweat with fear on a roller coaster or a Ferris wheel. The fear might not be a problem if the person simply avoids Ferris wheels and roller coasters, but it can be a big problem if their job requires them to work on the top floor of a high-rise building. "Every person has had a fear or fears at some time in their life and will do so in the future," Brindley wrote. "It is how we deal with those fears that makes the difference."[12] For people with a phobia, the urge to avoid the frightening object or situation overpowers other important things in their lives. When the trigger is truly unavoidable—for example, when someone with urophobia needs to urinate—they suffer severe distress the whole time they are dealing with it.

## Phobias Can Change Over Time

People tend to fear different things at different ages. Many infants have irrational fears of strangers or of anyone who is not their mother. At 18 months old, a toddler is most likely to fear being away from their parents.

Children who are four to six years old tend to be afraid of imaginary things, such as monsters or ghosts. These fears generally disappear once children stop believing in the creatures. However, if this does not happen, the fear can stick with them as they age. For example, many adults who say they have experienced an encounter with a ghost have a phobia of ghosts.

By age seven, a person's fears typically shift to something more specific that can actually happen, such as a fear of getting caught in a storm, being bitten by a dog, or falling off a bicycle.

Around age 12, common fears shift again, focusing mainly on social phobias. Fear of giving presentations in class, taking tests in front of a teacher, or going to school at all tend to crop up at about this age. Teenagers' changing hormone levels play a role in these, and once they have finished puberty and their hormone levels have stabilized, they tend to lose these phobias.

For some adults, childhood fears do not vanish, and there is no real way to predict who will or will not outgrow their phobias. However, experts say that the older the fear, the harder it is to treat and eliminate it, so confronting it early on before it becomes a phobia is important.

## Multiple Factors

The root causes of a phobia are not always clear. Certain experiences, however, do seem to spark certain fear responses. Many people who have specific phobias can name the incident that first frightened them.

Julia Ruddick, a woman who has koumpounophobia (fear of buttons), can trace this back to one childhood experience. "I've had this problem ever since I was a little girl," she said. "It began after I opened a drawer at home one day and saw a green cardigan with big buttons that gave me the creeps."[13] Apple co-founder Steve Jobs pioneered touchscreens because he, too, had koumpounophobia and did not want to have to touch buttons on his electronic devices. Another woman, Karen, linked her fear of restaurants to an illness she had as a teenager:

> *It started when I was 14 and recovering from glandular fever. I hadn't been able to eat properly for several months so as soon as I could eat proper meals I went for it. But my stomach had shrunk so I couldn't swallow all the food I was trying to cram in. After one particularly heavy meal, I had to run off to be sick. I was really ashamed and embarrassed, and I became so frightened of it happening again that I started avoiding eating in public.*[14]

Getting attacked by a dog, coming down with an illness, or being trapped in a violent storm are other experiences that can set off a lifelong specific phobia. Even some of the least common phobias tend to stem from a traumatic incident; for example, someone who endured abuse as a child by being tied up may develop linonophobia (fear of string). This is known as conditioning, where someone learns over time to associate an object or situation with the feeling of fear. However, other people have phobias that do not relate to a specific incident—at least, not one the person can remember. Sometimes a person learns to be afraid of something because their parent has a phobia of that thing; for example, someone whose mother fears spiders may also fear spiders. People who have generally anxious parents or other close relatives are also more likely to experience anxiety and develop phobias, suggesting that it is partially a learned behavior.

Environmental factors are only part of the picture, though. Most experts agree that genetics probably also play a role in the development of phobias. Studies of identical twins have strengthened this theory. Identical twins have deoxyribonucleic acid (DNA)—the material that carries genetic information—that is essentially identical because they are formed when one fertilized egg splits into two in the womb. Fraternal twins are formed when two separate eggs are fertilized in the womb, so their DNA is similar but not identical.

One 2008 study conducted in Sweden followed 1,245 pairs of twins from the ages of 8 to 20. Periodically, they were mailed questionnaires about their fears. The scientific journal *Nature* reported, "At every age a child was more likely to be fearful if their identical twin was too. Fraternal twins also shared a tendency towards fearfulness but the link was less strong, indicating a genetic component to fearfulness."[15] By comparing the twins' responses at different ages, researchers were also able to determine that the respondents' fears changed over time, indicating that different genes affecting fear are active at different points in a person's life. While the study did not identify specific fear genes,

Children learn many things from watching their parents, even if they are not directly told these things. Some of these are positive, such as learning to enjoy healthy foods. Others are negative, such as developing anxious habits.

other researchers are conducting separate studies on fear genes.

## PTSD and Phobias

It can be difficult for mental health professionals to tell whether someone is experiencing PTSD or a phobia after a traumatic incident, since the symptoms tend to be similar. PTSD is "a complex psychological reaction to extreme stress or trauma. For PTSD to develop, the sufferer must have been exposed to a situation in which grave physical harm was present or threatened."[1] This can include car crashes, injuries, and abuse. Phobias can also develop after traumatic events. For example, people with ablutophobia (fear of bathing) may develop their fear after a near-death experience involving water, and those with pogonophobia (fear of beards) may have had a traumatic encounter with a bearded man.

The difference between PTSD and a phobia is that PTSD is more severe and has more symptoms, including nightmares about the traumatic event; unwanted, distressing memories called flashbacks throughout the day; difficulty sleeping; feeling jumpy and irritable for seemingly no reason; and persistent feelings of fear, horror, guilt, or shame relating to the event. However, separating PTSD from a phobia or even from GAD, which can also result from a traumatic event, is further complicated by the fact that not everyone with PTSD has all the symptoms and by the fact that it is possible—in fact, very common—to have multiple anxiety disorders at once. People should not try to diagnose themselves or anyone else; instead, if they are experiencing distressing symptoms that could be PTSD, a phobia, or GAD, they should speak to a mental health expert.

1. Lisa Fritscher, "What You Need to Know About PTSD and Phobias," Verywell Mind, October 3, 2018. www.verywellmind.com/ptsd-and-phobias-2671927.

Some people's phobias are set off by something they have read about in a newspaper or seen on television. For instance, many people are afraid of flying in an airplane because they have heard about plane crashes. Statistics consistently indicate that air travel is safer than any other traveling method, but some people tend to think air travel is more dangerous because plane crashes are reported on more frequently than car crashes. Social psychologists call this the availability heuristic—"a mental shortcut that helps you make fast, but sometimes incorrect, assessments ... If you can quickly think of multiple examples of something happening ... you will believe that it is more common."[16] However, most people use the availability heuristic at one point or another, and it is unknown why some of these people develop a phobia and others do not.

## Leading Causes of Death in Perspective (Britain)

war
pregnancy & birth
medical complications
murder
undetermined events
mental health disorders
transport accidents
suicide
musculoskeletal disorders
diabetes
non-transport accidents
infections
kidney disorders
digestive disorders
nervous system disorders

heart & circulatory disorders

cancer

respiratory disorders

Murders are reported in the news far more frequently than deaths from a disease such as a respiratory disorder, but they actually happen far less frequently, as this information from the British National Health Service shows. Because of the use of the availability heuristic, people tend to be more afraid of being murdered than developing a problem with their lungs.

It is also unclear why some people develop a phobia and others do not even after experiencing something frightening first-hand. For example, some people who have survived a car crash can continue to travel in cars without fear, while other people are terrified of being in a car crash even if they have never experienced one. To better understand why some people have phobias and others do not, doctors and scientists are exploring the symptoms and the experiences of terror that set phobias apart from realistic fears.

## CHAPTER THREE

# LIFE WITH PHOBIAS

Phobias are incredibly common, but frequently misunderstood. Many people talk about their phobias in terms of fear, blurring the lines between a natural feeling and a mental illness. For example, someone with coulrophobia may say, "I'm afraid of clowns." Clowns unnerve many people, which is why they are commonly seen in horror movies. For example, Stephen King's classic novel *It* is about a predatory, shapeshifting creature that primarily takes on the appearance of an evil clown named Pennywise. The creature lives in the sewers and lures children to their deaths. Since 1986, when the novel was published, *It* has been made into two movies—the original miniseries in 1990 and a two-part remake, with the first movie released in 2017 and the second in 2019. Both of these variations on the same story show that horrifying clowns resonate with many people. However, someone with a true phobia of clowns would likely not be able to watch the movie, as they would not feel enjoyably frightened or "creeped out," but rather panicked.

"Panic" is another word for the fight-or-flight response that is automatic in all mammals, not just humans. When faced with a life-or-death situation, the body takes over, and logic disappears.

## The Brain's Stress Response

The brain is not one single mass. It is made up of

Shown here is Pennywise, the villain from Stephen King's *It*.

several different structures that interact with each other and have distinct functions. The area that deals with stress, called the limbic system, is found deep inside the brain; it is essentially the same in all mammals, and it controls the most basic survival behaviors, producing responses that a person does not consciously control.

Within this part of the brain are the thalamus, hippocampus, amygdala, and hypothalamus. These structures work together to determine which emotions are attached to the things the ears, eyes, and other sensory organs perceive; for instance, whether the person at the door seems dangerous or friendly.

The thalamus lies in the center of the limbic system and serves as the gateway between the outside world and the inner brain. It is the central relay point where information from the senses comes in and is distributed to the appropriate parts of the brain. It screens information and determines what is and what is not important to react to.

The hippocampus is a sausage-shaped organ that puts data into context. It connects the information the senses perceive with other information already in the brain. It organizes memories, retrieves them when necessary, and sends memories out to the appropriate places in the cerebrum for long-term storage. It helps people have a sense of place and time—lets them know what is the past, present, and future and how to relate new information to past information.

The amygdala is an almond-shaped structure about 1 inch (2.54 cm) long that is involved in learning and memory. It regulates emotions and connects them—especially fear and aggression—to a stimulus. For example, rats that have had their amygdalae removed show no fear and calmly approach cats, unaware of their danger.

The hypothalamus is small, but it directs a lot of important functions. It controls the neurotransmitters that control the endocrine system—the glands that make hormones. The pituitary gland, which is located within the hypothalamus, is the most important of these glands. Because it controls the activity of all the other glands, it can make a person feel anger, sadness, or happiness. It triggers the adrenaline rush one might experience during an accident or a roller coaster ride. It also controls the fight-or-flight response—the split-second reaction that happens when a person must decide whether to fight or run from danger.

All these structures are connected through a complex system of nerve cells. These communicate with each other and the rest of the body through chemical messengers called neurotransmitters and hormones. Neurotransmitters are chemicals released by nerve cells, or neurons, to pass information from cell to cell. There are many neurotransmitters, and they act within the synapses, or spaces, between nerve cells. Hormones are chemicals released by glands; for instance, the adrenal glands release adrenaline—also called epinephrine—which heightens awareness and increases reaction time when someone is nervous or excited. Neurotransmitters travel a relatively small distance from one neighboring neuron to another, while hormones travel through the bloodstream throughout the body to reach the cells they target.

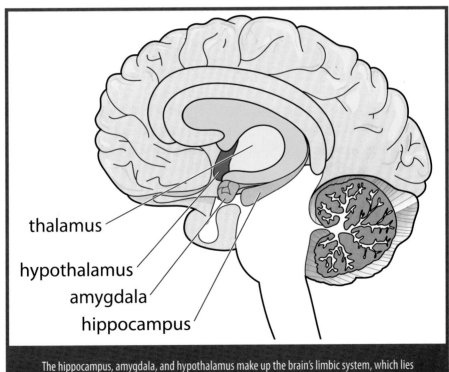

thalamus

hypothalamus

amygdala

hippocampus

The hippocampus, amygdala, and hypothalamus make up the brain's limbic system, which lies on both sides of the thalamus. The limbic system controls emotions, memories, and instincts.

The hippocampus determines what the information the senses send it means. It could be the sound of a gunshot, movement in a dark alley, or the feeling of a snake slithering against the skin. The hippocampus evaluates whether the sensation has been experienced before, what the sensation previously meant, and what other sensory details are present. If the hippocampus perceives a threat to survival, then the amygdala switches on the fear response and tells the hypothalamus to sound the alarm.

When activated, the hypothalamus releases corticotropin-releasing factor (CRF), which switches on two brain-body connections—the sympathetic nervous system (SNS) and the adrenocortical system—that prepare the body to respond to the threat.

The SNS works on nerve pathways throughout the body to send messages. It sends out impulses to glands and muscles and tells the adrenal glands, located just above the kidneys, to pump epinephrine, norepinephrine, and other hormones into the bloodstream. Instantly, the heart beats faster, and the bronchial tubes in the lungs open wider for easier breathing. Blood pressure rises to pump more oxygen-rich blood to the brain and to the muscles in the arms and legs.

At the same time, the CRF switches on the pituitary gland, which pumps adrenocorticotropic hormone (ACTH) into the bloodstream. It travels through the blood to activate the adrenal glands so they release cortisol and other hormones. Cortisol keeps the initial burst of energy high and keeps the blood pressure elevated for a longer period of time. Certain body functions that are not necessary during an emergency, such as digestion, are temporarily shut down to conserve energy for running or fighting. Once the threat is gone, the brain releases a different set of chemical messengers to halt the stress response, bringing the body back to a normal resting state.

# Unusual Phobias

Hundreds of specific phobias have been named, and hundreds more are still being named, although not all of them are officially recognized by the APA. Some are relatively common, such as pediophobia (fear of dolls). However, many of them are very rare, including:

- arachibutyrophobia: fear of peanut butter getting stuck to the roof of the mouth
- basophobia: fear of walking
- bibliophobia: fear of books
- cacophobia: fear of ugly things
- decidophobia: fear of making decisions
- ephebiphobia: fear of young people
- ergophobia: fear of work
- euphobia: fear of getting good news
- genuphobia: fear of knees
- hippopotomonstrosesquippedaliophobia: fear of long words
- leukophobia: fear of the color white
- lutraphobia: fear of otters
- macrophobia: fear of long waits
- octophobia: fear of the number eight
- perdetophobia: fear of not saving work before the computer crashes
- syngenesophobia: fear of relatives
- turophobia: fear of cheese
- xylophobia: fear of wood

Most people think otters are cute, but those with lutraphobia avoid them. Otters, like any wild animal, will attack when they are distressed, so people with this phobia may have developed it after either being bitten by an otter or seeing it happen to someone else.

All of this is useful when someone is facing a true threat, such as a dangerous animal. However, for people with a phobia, it becomes a problem because they panic at things that are not likely to hurt them. This interferes with daily life because someone who is panicking cannot think about anything but their fear. Symptoms of a panic attack include hyperventilation (breathing too fast), excessive sweating, trembling, dizziness, nausea, and clenched muscles. However, not everyone experiences panic the exact same way; some people are able to hide their panic attack, while others have symptoms that are easily observed by those around them.

## Creating a Feedback Loop

Panic reinforces phobias, creating what is called a feedback loop. Journalist Susan Stevens explained, "Once you panic, your physical reaction is etched into memory so you'll be ready for a similar threat in the future." For people with a phobia, Stevens said, this memory "primes them to respond excessively to harmless situations."[17]

Unnecessary panic takes a toll on a person's health, both physical and mental. After adrenaline leaves the body, the person generally feels shaky and tired. Prolonged periods of stress or panic, which keep adrenaline in the body for longer than necessary, can harm the heart by making it beat faster than it is supposed to. Adrenaline also makes people have difficulty sleeping, which can cause further health problems.

Another contributor to the feedback loop is embarrassment. People with a phobia typically know their panic reaction is out of proportion to the danger posed by the trigger. When they calm down, they often feel embarrassed for panicking, even though they could not help it. This causes them to avoid their phobia trigger even more so they do not panic and feel embarrassed again.

Many people feel embarrassed after a panic attack because they believe they should have been able to prevent themselves from overreacting. This can make them even more determined to avoid their phobia trigger.

Although people with a phobia avoid their trigger whenever possible, a common misconception is that everyone with a phobia is physically incapable of confronting their trigger. If it is absolutely necessary, many people can deal with the thing that frightens them—especially if their phobia is not severe—although they will feel high levels of anxiety the whole time. One example of this came up in 2018 after Dr. Christine Blasey Ford accused Supreme Court Justice (then nominee) Brett Kavanaugh of sexually assaulting her when they were in high school. The Senate Judiciary Committee held a hearing on September 27 to determine Kavanaugh's fitness for the Supreme

Court, calling upon both Ford and Kavanaugh to testify. During Ford's testimony, she was questioned about her fear of flying by Rachel Mitchell, a sex-crimes prosecutor. Mitchell asked how Ford got to Washington, D.C. for the hearing, and Ford replied that she flew there:

> *Mitchell: I ask that because it's been reported by the press that you would not submit to an interview with the committee because of your fear of flying. Is that true?*
>
> *Ford: Well, I was willing—I was hoping they would come to me. But then realized that was an unrealistic request ... So, that was certainly what I was hoping, was to avoid having to get on an airplane. But I eventually was able to get up the gumption with the help of some friends, and get on the plane.*[18]

Ford has also traveled in the past for both work and fun, which made many people accuse her of lying about her fear because she was not acting in a way they believed a person with a true phobia would act. However, it has been pointed out that people with phobias are often treated inconsistently:

> *In January 2014, survivors of US Airways Flight 1549 gathered in New York to celebrate the so-called Miracle on the Hudson. Among the attendees was Clay Presley, a businessman who "decided to conquer that fear [of flying] by getting a pilot's license," the New York Post wrote. Presley was celebrated for facing his fears and getting out of his comfort zone. Ford, pushing past hers, was essentially asked why she didn't stay home.*[19]

Embarrassment and the fear of not being believed makes it hard for many people with specific phobias to get help for their problem because they find it difficult to explain their phobia to someone. It can be difficult for someone with a phobia to describe what it is about the trigger that scares them; in fact, they may be unsure themselves. This was realistically portrayed in the novel *Harry Potter and the Chamber of Secrets* when the character of Ron Weasley tried to explain to his friends what it was about spiders that bothered him:

> *"I—don't—like—spiders," said Ron tensely.*
>
> *"I never knew that," said Hermione, looking at Ron in surprise. "You've used spiders in Potions loads of times …"*
>
> *"I don't mind them dead," said Ron, who was carefully looking anywhere but at the window. "I just don't like the way they move …"*
>
> *Hermione giggled.*
>
> *"It's not funny," said Ron fiercely … Hermione was obviously still trying not to laugh.*[20]

When others laugh at people with phobias, as Hermione does to Ron, it makes this problem worse. For this reason, the person may instead choose to suffer quietly instead of seeking help.

Doctors think that many specific phobias go unreported for exactly this reason—people do not want to admit to fears that they know are not sensible. Instead, they go through life quietly hoping that they do not have an embarrassing run-in with their phobia trigger. Unfortunately, this causes unnecessary daily stress and constant feelings of dread as they fear an unexpected encounter with their trigger. Therapists are trained to deal with many problems that do not seem sensible to others and know how to help someone with their phobia without laughing at them for it.

## Supporting a Loved One

Phobias can be confusing to friends and family members who do not suffer from one. They may not understand what is so scary about things such as balloons or rabbits; they may even try to expose the person to their phobia, either because they find the person's scared reaction to be funny or because they believe they are helping the person get over their fear. For example, a parent may insist that their child with cynophobia must pet someone's dog so they can see that there is nothing to be afraid of. In reality, it is cruel to make a person with a phobia confront their fear, especially without warning. Although loved ones may believe they are helping, there are specific ways mental health experts go about helping someone with a phobia deal with their trigger. Simply thrusting the person in front of their trigger does not cure the phobia; it only reinforces it. A better way to help someone with a phobia is to encourage them to seek treatment, let them know their feelings are valid, and remind them that they are loved.

It is important for friends and family to let a loved one with a phobia know that they will be supportive but will not regularly put their lives on hold. It is equally important for the person with a phobia to recognize when they are asking for something unreasonable and not to blame their support system for not caring enough or not doing enough. For example, someone with monophobia (fear of being alone) may depend completely on others to stay with them to prevent them from panicking. This has the effect of isolating the loved one along with the person with monophobia. Advice columnist Jennifer Peepas, who blogs under the name Captain Awkward, pointed out that "there is no mental health condition ... that is treated or accommodated by the people around you being endlessly compliant ... to the detriment of their own well-being and happiness."[21] This is why therapy is an important tool: Managing emotions and taking personal responsibility is difficult and sometimes painful, and therapy can help people learn this skill.

Some people feel as though their phobia makes them difficult to be around. A great way for people to support them is to remind them they are still loved.

## Poor Coping Mechanisms

When someone does not tell anyone about their phobia and does not seek treatment for it, they struggle because they lack emotional support. Even if a few people know about the phobia, sometimes the feelings of fear and dread become so strong that it seems like too much for the person to handle. When this happens, the person sometimes turns to drugs or alcohol. People who have social phobias, "more than patients with any other anxiety disorder, say that they use alcohol and certain drugs to relieve anxiety,"[22] according to psychiatrist John R. Marshall. They believe it is helping them, but in reality, substance abuse does not solve problems—it only causes them. For a person with a social phobia who also struggles with alcohol addiction, getting help for either problem is twice as hard. During Alcoholics Anonymous (AA) meetings, which are supposed to help people get over their addiction to drinking, people in the group take turns talking about themselves. Doing this while sober, which is required during such a meeting, can be awful for someone with a fear of speaking in public.

## Celebrities with Phobias

Even celebrities are not immune to phobias. For example, film director Martin Scorsese suffers from aviophobia, refusing to travel in a plane unless he can first work out safe weather patterns for the flight path. If he cannot conclude without a doubt that there will be a good landing, then he will not risk flying. Other celebrities with phobias include:

• Nicole Kidman, who avoids butterflies at all costs

• Matthew McConaughey, who gets anxious whenever he is near a revolving door

• Adele, who has been afraid of seagulls since she was nine years old

• Cameron Diaz, who is so afraid of doorknobs that she will not touch them

• Megan Fox, who will not touch paper that is not laminated

• Nicki Minaj, who refuses to use escalators

It is not clear whether some of these phobias have been diagnosed by a medical professional, but it is clear that they all cause severe anxiety in the people they affect.

People who self-medicate often turn to drugs and alcohol because they are unwilling or unable to seek help. Although more awareness has been brought to anxiety disorders and other mental illnesses in recent years, many people still feel a stigma, or negative view, around seeing a therapist. They may believe that only people with serious mental illnesses see therapists, and they may also try to tell themselves that their personal phobia is not serious and that they can handle it on their own. However, they are often in denial about how bad their situation is.

Other people may not seek help because of the cost. In the United States, there are many complex factors that go into health insurance prices and coverage, but most people agree that insurance prices are higher than the average American can afford, even if an employer is paying part of the premium (monthly cost). They are higher than in any other developed country in the world, and many insurance plans set limits on what is covered. The lower the monthly premium, the fewer things are covered and the higher the out-of-pocket cost for things that are covered, so someone who chooses a plan with a lower premium may not be paying less in the long term.

Many insurance plans cover prescription medications but do not cover therapy to treat mental illness or stress. Even when they do, many therapists do not accept insurance because they find the insurance system difficult and confusing to manage. For this reason, people may not seek therapy because they feel they are unable to afford it. However, some therapists offer treatment on a sliding scale, meaning that they charge what the client can afford. Research into therapy takes some time and effort, but people who have benefited from treatment often say that it is well worth it.

It is not unusual for people to try to hide weaknesses or even deny problems altogether, but a person experiencing a phobia needs to understand that this is a potentially serious mental condition, not something shameful that needs to be hidden. The person should seek help rather than trying to hide the condition. Like the flu or any other illness, without the right kind of medical help, phobias can become much worse. Not taking the proper steps to treat one can result in poor performance at school, loss of employment, friendships, family relationships, and—in the worst cases—people's lives. If a phobia that causes a lot of distress goes untreated long enough, some people eventually feel that life is simply too hard and try to commit suicide. However, phobias are a problem that can be treated.

## CHAPTER FOUR

# THERAPY AND OTHER TREATMENTS

When a phobia becomes so severe and constant that it interferes with a person's life—either by affecting their choices or keeping their stress levels high—then it becomes necessary for the person to seek treatment. Unfortunately, psychiatrist Gavin Andrews wrote, "Phobias are difficult to treat because sufferers are slow to come for treatment and often afraid of confronting their fears when they get to treatment."[23] The most effective treatment for a phobia involves confronting the fear a little at a time, and even the thought of doing this can be enough to make someone panic. Many people convince themselves that their phobias are not bad enough to need treatment and only end up going to therapy when something convinces them that they are in denial. This could be something such as a friend letting them know their phobia is getting out of control, or it could be an event related directly to the phobia—for example, someone with aviophobia may end up missing out on a great job opportunity because they refuse to get on a plane.

Social phobias and agoraphobia can be especially distressing. While a fear of thunderstorms or air travel does not necessarily make a normal life impossible, a phobia of using the telephone or of being farther than three blocks from home can soon start to affect a person's lifestyle. Social phobias and agoraphobia can take a huge toll on happiness and success.

People who are afraid of talking on the phone often do not make important appointments for themselves. This can have a negative effect on their overall health and happiness.

One of the barriers to treatment is the stigma that still exists around mental health treatment. Due to widespread media attention, it is less strong than it was in the past, but it still exists. Since phobias are treated by psychiatrists and psychologists, needing to see one of these professionals can be embarrassing in itself to some people. People with phobias may be afraid that others will think they are "crazy." However, people who have worked up the nerve to seek treatment say it has improved their lives immensely.

# Finding the Right Therapist

Being misunderstood is only one of the reasons why some people live with their fear for a long time before they consider seeking help. Sometimes they try going to therapy or talking to a medical doctor only to find that the person they chose does not have a good understanding of phobias. For example, psychiatrist John R. Marshall described a day when he was a guest on a call-in radio program. He was sure that people listening at home would pick up the phone and tell him about their social fears, but nobody called. Marshall did not understand why.

"On the air, I remarked that I was surprised, and even a little disappointed, that most of the people who called in seemed to have anxiety-related disorders other than social phobia," Marshall wrote. "On my next day in the clinic, one of my socially phobic patients told me she had heard me on the radio. 'And if others are like me, there is no way you could have expected them to call in,'" she told him. "I would never dream of calling in to a radio program. That would only multiply my chances of making a complete fool of myself—astronomically."[24]

Finding the right therapist can be a challenge. Because of the wide variety of mental illnesses, not every therapist is equipped to deal with every problem. Even if a particular therapist is experienced in dealing with phobias, sometimes their personality clashes with the patient's. There is no one right method or person for everyone. A person with a phobia may start going to one therapist and find that they do not like or trust that person. It is perfectly acceptable for someone to choose a different therapist whose personality and approach to the problem fits with the patient's wants and needs. For example, some patients may want to joke around about their problems, while others want to speak about them very seriously. Finding a therapist who can match the patient's tone is very important in this case. It is up to the patient to do research, ask questions, and trust their instincts when it comes to finding a therapist. Finding the right person may be a stressful and time-consuming task, but therapy is no use if the patient is not comfortable with the person they are working with, so it is well worth the effort. Asking a friend or trusted adult to help may make the process easier.

Some red flags, or bad signs, to consider when searching for a therapist to help with phobias include:

- They do not discuss the patients' rights in the first session and do not have the patient sign a confidentiality agreement.
- They do not have experience helping people with phobias.
- They recommend things that go against what the patient believes in.
- They do not answer any questions or give confusing or conflicting answers.
- They share too much information about their own lives.
- The patient does not feel progress is being made after several sessions.
- They roll their eyes, make rude comments, say things sarcastically, or do other things to make the patient feel judged or shamed.
- They do not remember basic things about the patient (for example, getting the patient's name wrong).
- They answer phone calls, emails, or texts during the session.
- The patient feels so uncomfortable with the therapist (not with the process of working through their phobias) that they start thinking about skipping sessions.

Patients should feel comfortable enough with their therapist to speak up when something is not working. It is important to remember that patients are allowed to switch therapists at any time if they feel their current therapist is not the right fit for them.

Doctors are realizing how important it is to help society understand phobias. If more people understood their own phobias and felt comfortable getting help, perhaps more would turn to doctors instead of letting the problem get worse or self-medicating with drugs and alcohol. Treating phobias early is very important, because the longer a person lives with a phobia, the worse it is likely to get. The worse it gets, the more damage is done to someone's life.

## Medication: Useful but Limited

There is no medication that can cure a phobia, but there are some that can treat the symptoms long enough to help someone deal with their fear, especially in cases where it is necessary for them to confront their trigger. To treat the underlying phobia, it is sometimes necessary to stop the panic response first. Medications that relax the person first can help.

"When your anxiety level is very high, or when you've been avoiding particular situations for a long time," wrote author Edmund J. Bourne, "you may, quite literally, have difficulty 'getting out the door.'" These are the situations in which medication might be useful. "While not providing a long-term solution," Bourne continued, "medication can sometimes help you get over the initial blocks and barriers to getting started."[25]

Medications are only a portion of the treatment for a phobia. There is no pill someone with arachnophobia can take to prevent being afraid of spiders, and some of the medications prescribed to treat the anxiety a phobia causes are only meant for short-term use. One type of medication frequently given to phobia patients is called a beta-blocker, which blocks the effects of epinephrine, or adrenaline. This means a person does not feel the physical effects of anxiety, such as increased heart rate, sweating, and trembling. However, beta-blockers do nothing to treat anxious thoughts, so they are not helpful for everyone. According to *University Health News*, "when you face your fear, whatever it is, without having the physical symptoms you normally associate with fear, eventually that fear often diminishes or even goes away [altogether]. Because of this, beta blockers can be beneficial in combination with cognitive behavior therapy ... in order to help people overcome specific fears and phobias."[26] In a 2015 study on arachnophobia and beta-blockers, researchers found that giving participants one dose of the beta-blocker propranolol made them less likely to avoid spiders for at least a year. Side effects of beta-blockers may include fatigue, weight gain, dizziness, and cold hands.

A second class of medication that can be used for phobias is called benzodiazepines. These are anti-anxiety medications that relax a person almost to the point of sleepiness, making them less likely to feel anxious. They work by increasing the effectiveness of a neurotransmitter called gamma-aminobutyric acid (GABA), which calms the brain. This group of drugs can be given orally or through a vein in extreme cases when the patient needs to be sedated. Diazepam (Valium), alprazolam (Xanax), clonazepam (Klonopin), and lorazepam (Ativan) are the most commonly prescribed benzodiazepines. They are helpful for situations where a person is required to face their fear; for example, they can calm someone with aviophobia long enough to help them get through their flight or help someone with a fear of public speaking get through a work presentation.

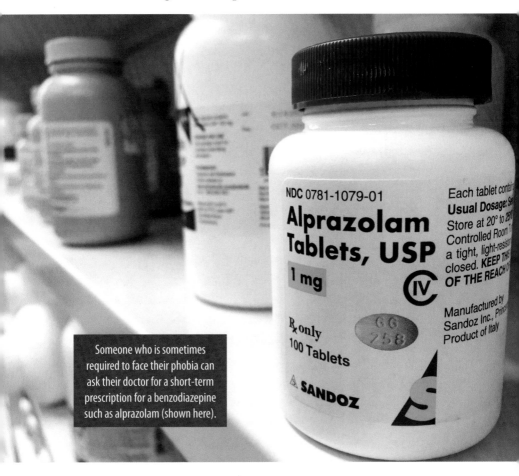

Someone who is sometimes required to face their phobia can ask their doctor for a short-term prescription for a benzodiazepine such as alprazolam (shown here).

However, benzodiazepines are neither a long-term solution nor a good solution for a phobia a person encounters frequently. This is because they can be addictive and dangerous. If the patient takes them longer than a few weeks or takes more pills at one time than recommended, they can become both physically and psychologically dependent upon and addicted to the drugs. Their body has become used to, or tolerant of, the drugs, and this means that to produce the same results, the patient will need stronger and stronger doses. When someone has developed an addiction to any drug, either prescribed or illegal, they have to go through an uncomfortable and difficult time called withdrawal to break free of the drug. Symptoms of benzodiazepine withdrawal syndrome include confusion, loss of appetite, shaking, sweating, insomnia, and ringing in the ears. Additionally, taking them with alcohol can kill the user.

All of these medications have their uses and drawbacks, and not every medication is right for every person. A doctor should always be consulted before someone tries a new medication, and they should never take a medication that has been prescribed to someone else.

## Alternative Therapies

Some people cannot take certain medications because of the way they interact with other medications they are already taking. Others simply do not like the idea of taking pills. Taking medication to calm down is a personal choice; each person must discuss the idea with their doctor or therapist to decide what is right for them. People who cannot or will not take medication may find relief in practices such as massage, meditation, and aromatherapy.

Massage therapy and aromatherapy can be particularly helpful in decreasing consistently high levels of anxiety. If someone has to have frequent contact with their phobia trigger, they will likely be anxious much of the time. Massage therapy has been shown to lower anxiety and stress and decrease the hormones that cause stress. In a study conducted at the Touch Research Institute at the University of Miami School of Medicine, one group of subjects was given chair massages twice a week for five weeks. The control group—the group of people who did not receive massages—was directed to simply relax in the massage chairs for 15 minutes. Both groups were monitored by means of an electroencephalogram (EEG) before, during, and after the study period. An EEG measures changes in the brain, so researchers could see how people's brain activity changed in response to either getting or not getting a massage. The participants were rated on several psychological scales before and after the study period. In addition to a marked lowering of anxiety levels, the group receiving the massages showed enhanced alertness and increased speed and accuracy in math skills over the control group. This study indicates that massage therapy benefits people not only by relieving anxiety, but also by improving mental alertness.

Aromatherapy also appears to benefit some people by lowering anxiety. According to aromatherapists, using certain fragrant substances in lotions and sprays can improve mood and overall general health. Some scents, such as lavender and sandalwood, seem to have a calming effect on people. Aromatherapists believe that the use of these products can enhance the beneficial effects of other types of treatment by helping the patient relax.

Many people also find meditation or visualization helpful, and unlike massage therapy or aromatherapy, it can be done anywhere. For example, if someone with arachnophobia encounters a spider and feels close to having a panic attack, they can close their eyes for a few minutes, take deep, slow breaths, and imagine themselves in a calming situation, such as on a beach or in front of a campfire—whatever works for that particular person.

Physical activity is also a proven way to increase

Visualization exercises—for example, closing the eyes and imagining relaxing on a beach—can help someone control their panic response.

the amount of endorphins and serotonin in the brain. While serotonin sends chemical "feel good" messages to the brain, endorphins act as natural painkillers in the body. Together, these substances lower stress and anxiety and cause a feeling of well-being. Just 30 to 40 minutes of aerobic exercise 3 or 4 times a week stimulates the body's production of these chemicals. The exercise can be walking, jogging, bicycling, playing tennis, aerobics, or swimming. Exercise reduces muscle tension, one effect of stress and anxiety. Exercise is also a healthy outlet for the fight-or-flight state of mind caused by anxiety, so it could be a helpful way for someone to work off the adrenaline rush that accompanies facing their phobia. In addition to raising levels of stress-lowering hormones, exercise also lowers levels of chemicals in the body that increase stress. Physical activity is also good for maintaining overall health, and people generally feel better mentally when they feel good physically. Along the same lines, people should try to get enough sleep each night and eat a healthy diet. People who are especially anxious should avoid caffeine and overly sugary foods, which have been shown to increase anxiety.

Additionally, some people report that chamomile tea has a calming effect. Studies show that it can make people feel more sleepy and relaxed, possibly because of a substance in the tea that binds to benzodiazepine receptors in the brain. However, since chamomile is an herb, the effects will not be as powerful as a pharmaceutical drug.

Some people have strong opinions on whether or not pharmaceutical drugs are helpful. Many people believe that natural therapies are better, although this is not always the case; some synthetic, or man-made, medications are very useful, just as some plants are poisonous. Additionally, dietary supplements are not regulated by the U.S. Food and Drug Administration (FDA), so the companies that make these products are not required to warn people about any possible side effects.

Some people choose not to take synthetic medications because they find that they feel worse on the medication than off it or because their phobia is mild enough or encountered infrequently enough that they do not require medication. Others find that their quality of life improves immensely when they take medication; they may get little or no benefit from aromatherapy or chamomile tea. Even for those who find alternative methods helpful, they may not completely eliminate stress and anxiety.

However, even a small reduction in the anxiety levels of a person with a phobia can be enough to help them start overcoming the phobia itself.

## Dealing with Fear

For most people, the first step in getting over a phobia is to develop the ability to be reasonable about it. This can potentially be achieved through cognitive behavioral therapy (CBT). People with phobias are far more afraid of their triggers than they logically should be, and CBT helps them learn new ways to cope with fear that make it seem less important.

During CBT for a phobia, a person practices thinking about fear differently. According to the Mayo Clinic, "You learn alternative beliefs about your fears and bodily sensations and the impact they've had on your life. CBT emphasizes learning to develop a sense of mastery and confidence with your thoughts and feelings rather than feeling overwhelmed by them."[27] For example, Courtney is a student who is terrified by the idea of everyone in her class staring at her and making fun of her if she walks in late. Her therapist might tell her to pay close attention to what happens when other students walk in late. Courtney may find relief and comfort in discovering that her classmates hardly notice a late student. She might then begin to realize that their reaction would be the same if she were to come in late. Coming to the realization that the thing she fears is not likely to happen could be an important step for Courtney in treating her phobia.

"In many cases," wrote psychologists Mark R. Leary and Robin M. Kowalski, "people's perceived self-presentation difficulties are more imagined than real. Socially anxious people also overestimate the degree to which their nervousness is apparent to other people."[28] For Courtney, realizing that her fear of being judged is all in her head and that her classmates are not watching her nearly as closely as she initially thought might be all she needs to start beating her phobia.

## Facing Phobias Directly

Getting over a phobia, according to the authors of *Mastering Your Fears and Phobias*, involves direct experience with the trigger in order to decrease the automatic fear response. "Treatment may last as little as one session or as many as 10, depending on the type of phobia," they wrote. "In our experience, animal phobias, blood phobias, and injection phobias often take fewer sessions."[29] These researchers have found that patients who are afraid of heights or of situations such as driving, for example, tend to take longer to treat.

This type of therapy is called exposure therapy because the person is being exposed to their phobia. Exposure therapy, which is a type of CBT, can be useful for someone who is already aware that their fear is out of proportion to the harmfulness of the trigger but who cannot stop themselves from having a panicked reaction to it. Exposure therapy has also been proven useful in treating other anxiety disorders, such as PTSD and OCD.

During exposure therapy, people face their fears head-on, but they do so slowly. Exposure to the thing that frightens them happens in small doses at first, depending on how much stress they can handle, making exposure therapy a series of baby steps toward beating a phobia. "Simply visualizing the feared object or activity might be enough to trigger the patient's fear at first," journalist Susan Stevens wrote. "Then therapy might involve looking at pictures or even virtual reality experiences until the patient can cope with the real thing."[30]

A person receiving behavioral therapy to treat a fear of fish, for example, might first spend time reading books about fish and studying pictures of them. In the beginning, even this might be enough to frighten them; however, later on in therapy, they might work up to visiting an aquarium and looking at real, living fish. Eventually, they might move on to touching a fish and then wading into a pool of water with a fish. By the end of therapy, the hope is that the person will be able to see or be near fish without experiencing panic and anxiety.

| Activity | Fear Level (0–100) |
|---|---|
| think about a spider | 10 |
| look at a photo of a spider | 25 |
| look at a real spider in a closed jar | 50 |
| hold the jar with the spider | 60 |
| let a spider crawl on your desk | 70 |
| let a spider crawl on your shoes | 80 |
| let a spider crawl on your pants leg | 90 |
| let a spider crawl on your sleeve | 95 |
| let a spider crawl on your bare arm | 100 |

Shown here is an example of what an exposure therapy plan might look like. The patient starts with the activities that cause the least fear. The idea is that, as they progress through the list, the fear level associated with the remaining activities decreases.

"It is helpful to confront the behaviors that one avoids, since doing more of what is feared often, though not always, tends to reduce anxiety,"[31] Marshall wrote. Exposure therapy is thought to be the best treatment for specific phobias—as long as the patient sticks with it through the initial anxiety.

Overcoming a fear of public speaking is one of the best-known uses of exposure therapy. Because stage fright is such a common fear, many different programs and classes are offered to help people put this problem behind them and face a positive future. J. Lyman MacInnis, author of *The Elements of Great Public Speaking*, believes that exposure to this fear through addressing small groups and progressing further along to speak before larger crowds is the only way to beat this social phobia. "Many people would list public speaking ahead of dying on a list of things they dread most," MacInnis wrote. "Early on you need to remember that you will eventually overcome your fear as you gain experience."[32]

In order to get treatment of any kind, however, someone must first do two things: admit their problem is serious enough to require medical intervention and seek out a medical professional to begin treatment. Reaching out for help and beginning treatment can be difficult, but the longer it is put off, the harder it will become.

## Increasing Understanding

Not everyone with a phobia likes to think they have a mental health problem due to the stigma that surrounds mental health in most societies. Additionally, some people are unaware that what they are experiencing is a phobia, so they do not think to seek help. For example, someone with a severe fear of public speaking may be told that this is a normal reaction that everyone experiences. Other people may be told they are just shy or antisocial. "There are effective treatments for panic disorder and the phobias," wrote psychiatrist Gavin Andrews. "The problem is that few people with these disorders attend treatment and, when they do, few are treated appropriately."[33] Because everyone is different, treatment for the same phobia may also differ from person to person, as doctors have discovered.

Educating the public about phobias, especially social phobias, is one way to get through to the many people who live with one and may not realize it. Doctors, too, need to better understand phobias. Unless they specialize in treating fears, many doctors might overlook the patient's phobia symptoms if they come in for something else. For instance, someone might go to the doctor because their heart was racing and they were short of breath, leading them to believe they were having a heart attack—a common thought when people experience a panic attack for the first time. The doctor might rule out a heart attack but might not ask the kinds of questions that could lead to diagnosing a phobia, such as how often those feelings had happened to the person in the past. People with an alcohol or drug addiction that developed as a result of self-medicating to cope with a phobia may also never be asked the kinds of questions that would help them identify the source of their problem. It can be helpful to individuals to keep track of how often they panic and what triggered it. If the panic attacks happen seemingly at random, the person may have panic disorder; if they avoid most or all social situations, they more likely have social anxiety disorder. If they do have a specific phobia, journaling can help them spot the pattern.

It might help if science could track down what

exactly causes some people to develop phobias while others do not. For example, not all people who have been bitten by a dog or stung by a bee develop a fear of dogs or bees, and not all people with dog or bee phobias have been bitten or stung, either. This is similar to PTSD in that not everyone who goes through a traumatic event develops the disorder. Additionally, PTSD and phobias share many symptoms. Looking to PTSD research might help scientists understand phobias better, since less research has been done into the causes of phobias. Researchers have identified several factors that increase a person's risk of getting PTSD. According to Dr. Rachel Yehuda, a PTSD specialist, "You're considered at risk if you have a family history of PTSD or other mood and anxiety disorders, if you've had adverse childhood experiences, or if you have a tendency to dissociate or panic."[34] Similarly, people who already have an anxiety disorder are at a higher risk for developing a phobia.

Children and teens are more likely than adults to develop PTSD, but research has focused less on these age groups because for a long time, it was believed only adults—mainly soldiers—got PTSD. Since people have to be over 18 to sign up or be drafted into the army, no one thought to study young people who had experienced trauma. Additionally, many researchers previously believed that children—especially those too young to fully understand what is happening around them— handle trauma better than adults and therefore could not be impacted by PTSD. However, a study reported by *TIME* magazine in 2010 found that not only do children and teens sometimes experience PTSD, they may be impacted more strongly when adults they trust are suffering similar symptoms. Additionally, young children are more likely to develop PTSD than older ones. Scientists suggest that a very young child may not have the capacity to deal with the high levels of stress because their brain is not yet fully formed. They also have not developed behavioral coping skills to handle a life-threatening trauma. Those skills are learned through the process of dealing with age-appropriate stresses and from watching parents and other adults. If this research holds true for phobias, it suggests that someone who suffers a traumatic event as a child is more likely to develop a phobia

Research has shown that children who experience a traumatic event such as a tornado are more likely to develop PTSD than adults who experience the same event. The same may be true of phobias as well, but more research is necessary to confirm this.

than someone who does not. However, the reasons why people develop a phobia without having a bad experience with their trigger remain a mystery.

## What Not to Say

Sometimes people try to be supportive of a loved one with a phobia, but what they think of as comforting words may actually be frustrating or upsetting to the person. Other times, people simply do not understand what someone with a phobia is going through, especially if the person's phobia is uncommon. Some things that are generally not helpful for someone with a phobia to hear include:

- "It's all in your head."
- "Calm down."
- "Just stop thinking about it."
- "I know how you feel; I don't like [trigger] much, either."
- "It can't hurt you."
- "If you actually have a phobia, how can you be near [trigger]?"
- "That's a ridiculous thing to be afraid of."
- "You're overreacting."
- "You would feel better if you [did yoga/meditated/ate healthier foods/etc.]."
- "A phobia isn't a mental illness. Everyone's scared of something."
- "Here, look at/touch [trigger]. You'll never get over it if you don't face it!"
- "Just try to tell yourself not to be scared."

Treatments for PTSD and phobias frequently overlap, and in fact, it is possible for someone to have both at the same time. It is also not uncommon for someone to have other mental disorders as well. When two or more disorders are present at the same time, they are called comorbidities. Depression is very often comorbid with anxiety disorders, including phobias, as well as schizophrenia and some eating disorders. This means that sometimes the challenge for doctors is trying to sort out exactly which disorders a person has and the best ways to treat each one.

## Problems Caused by Untreated Phobias

Unfortunately, mental illnesses such as phobias frequently go untreated. Experts report that this is especially true in the case of young adults. Teens may have difficulty communicating the seriousness of their problem to adults, or they may be dismissed as overly emotional and dramatic due to their changing hormones. A 2013 study conducted by Dr. E. Jane Costello, a researcher at Duke University, found that in the United States, "psychiatric disorders as a whole continue to be met with less seriousness than physical disabilities,"[35] causing people to believe there is no need to treat them. In reality, this can lead to worse problems later on, as the disorder gets harder to deal with and comorbidities develop.

Costello reported that only attention-deficit/ hyperactivity disorder (ADHD) is likely to be treated in teens: "While roughly 74 percent of children diagnosed with the disorder received treatment, those with phobias and anxiety only got professional help roughly 40 percent of the time."[36] Teens of color were less likely to receive help than white teens. As Costello pointed out, some people believe leaving a phobia or other mental disorder untreated is not as serious as leaving a physical disorder, such as diabetes or cancer, untreated. However, this is far from the truth. A phobia may not be physically painful, but it is mentally and emotionally exhausting and frustrating, especially if it is combined with a comorbidity. This can result in poor performance in school and taking too many sick days, which in turn can lead to difficulties graduating or finding a job later in life. This scenario could be more common than anyone realizes. Untreated phobias have big costs, both to individuals and to society. Based on her research, Costello recommended training more child psychiatrists to get to the root of mental issues early on.

# CHAPTER FIVE

# LOOKING FORWARD

Technology has advanced at an astounding pace in the last few decades. Many things have been invented that were once only part of science fiction stories, including video calling, touchscreens, holograms, 3-D printing, and virtual reality (VR) headsets. This last one has been used mainly for video games, but it is increasingly being used to treat phobias and PTSD.

VR is a computer-generated setting where people can participate and interact, to a certain degree, with an artificial or virtual environment. This technology involves many of the senses, including hearing, touch, sight, and sometimes even smell. A VR system has three parts. The first part is a fast, powerful computer called a reality simulator, which can run a VR program fast enough that there are no delays in interaction with the user. Within this simulator is the graphics board that produces the visual three-dimensional environment, the sound processors, and the controllers for the input and output devices that connect the user with the virtual environment. The second part consists of the input and output devices, called effectors. Effectors include head-mounted displays (HMD), joysticks, and wired gloves. The final part of the VR system is the user, or the person interacting with the virtual environment.

VR equipment was not widely available in the past, so it was not frequently used in therapy. When it was used, it was very expensive. However, in 2016, the Oculus Rift became available for use with video games. At about $500, it is still relatively expensive but much cheaper than VR sets were in the past. This could potentially make VR therapy much more affordable, since a therapist could buy one set and use it for multiple patients.

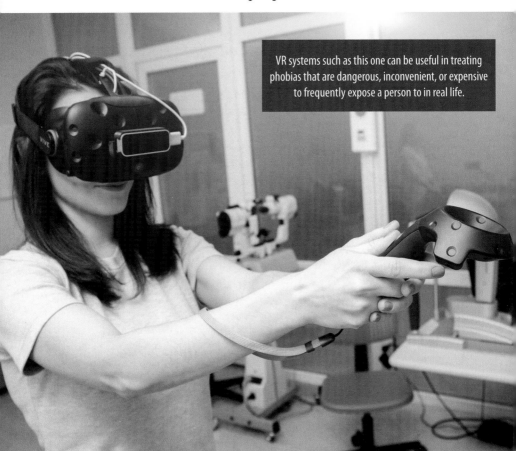

VR systems such as this one can be useful in treating phobias that are dangerous, inconvenient, or expensive to frequently expose a person to in real life.

## Why Use Cyber-Therapy?

There are many benefits to using VR therapy to treat phobias, especially flying, heights, driving, and animal phobias. For one thing, it is much safer. Someone with a fear of driving may panic when they first get behind the wheel of a car, causing them to drive unsafely and potentially hurting themselves or others. A VR headset or even a first-person driving game could simulate the experience of driving without putting anyone in danger. Another benefit is that the headset provides an experience that feels real but can be stopped at any time if it becomes too much for the patient to handle. For instance, someone with a fear of flying cannot simply step off the plane if they start to panic. VR therapy can allow the person to experience the environment of a plane as if they were really there, but the headset could be taken off at any point. The eventual goal

Getting too close to the edge of a cliff is dangerous even for someone without a fear of heights. VR therapy could help simulate this experience safely.

is to get the person to the point where they are comfortable enough to take an actual flight, but first it is necessary to desensitize them to the situation by repeatedly exposing them to it virtually.

VR can be helpful even for people without a dangerous phobia. For example, someone with a fear of public speaking could practice talking in front of a virtual crowd, which provides more realism than simply speaking in front of a photo of a crowd.

"For me, because of the nature of the feedback I received during the VRT sessions, I was able to identify my 'flying rough spots' easier," Kathy Feldman said. Previously, Feldman said, her fear of airline travel was so strong that she once abandoned her children on an airplane when she lost her courage to go through with her flight and ran back to the airport terminal. "Virtual Reality Therapy gave me more concrete feedback about what I, as a nervous flyer, needed to work through to begin flying again."[37]

Based on the idea of exposure therapy, VR sessions make it easy to start small and move to higher goals. For example, a person who has a phobia of spiders might begin with a session in which the VR helmet displays a realistic spider on the other side of a room. The next session might show a spider in a closed jar closer to the patient. In the third session, the jar might be open. Slowly, the patient is meant to build up enough courage to the point where they would be comfortable with the hypothetical idea of touching the spider. This is where VR therapy falls short, however—since the spider is virtual, it cannot actually be touched. Some things can only be experienced in real life.

Logically, the phobic patient undergoing VR therapy knows the whole time that they can remove the helmet and the virtual spider will go away. However, one of the defining characteristics of phobias is that they are not logical. Experts in this type of therapy have found that VR experiences cause the same feelings of panic that real-life exposure therapy sessions do, even though the person realizes the spider or other virtually produced fear is not really there. Thus, virtual exposure therapy allows patients to experience the thing they fear as if they were exposed to it in the real world.

VR therapists Max M. North, Sarah M. North, and Joseph R. Coble described one patient who

## Biofeedback

Therapists frequently combine VR exposure therapy with traditional CBT. Some also use biofeedback, which is a type of therapy that helps people control their body's typically involuntary responses. It is unclear exactly how or why biofeedback works, but research has shown that it lessens stress. During each session, electrodes are attached to the person's skin to monitor things such as their heart rate, breathing rate, blood pressure, and amount of sweat. The patient can watch these change in real time as they are exposed to something that makes them anxious. The biofeedback therapist teaches them relaxation exercises, including:

- Deep breathing

- Progressive muscle relaxation—alternately tightening and then relaxing different muscle groups

- Guided imagery—concentrating on a specific image (such as the color and texture of an orange) to focus your mind and make you feel more relaxed

- Mindfulness meditation—focusing your thoughts and letting go of negative emotions[1]

As the patient performs these techniques, they can watch their body's response on the monitor, getting instant feedback about how well they are working. The idea is to eventually get the patient to a point where they can use relaxation techniques wherever they are to quickly calm themselves.

1. "Overview of Biofeedback," WebMD, October 2, 2018. www.webmd.com/a-to-z-guides/biofeedback-therapy-uses-benefits#2.

finished a VR program to get rid of her fear of flying. By the end of her sessions, she faced the treatments with much less fear than she had in the beginning, but the researchers wanted to test how well she would respond if she actually took to the air.

"She was flown, in the company of the therapist, in a helicopter for approximately 10 minutes at low altitude over a beach on the Gulf of Mexico," they wrote. "As with the VRT sessions, she reported some anxiety at the beginning but rapidly grew more comfortable. Now the subject comfortably flies for long distances and experiences much less anxiety."[38]

A high-tech helmet and a special computer program can do wonders for people with specific phobias. Although it may not completely eliminate all fear, it can aid in pinpointing exactly what frightens them and how much of it they can handle before panicking. Scientists have found that virtual technology can also help people with a fear of less specific things, such as public humiliation or having a panic attack.

## There's an App for That

VR is not the only advanced technology that has been used to help people deal with phobias and other anxiety disorders. Some apps have also been created, including:

- ANA Takeoff Mode, which helps relax people during the takeoff of a flight. It keeps users distracted by making them solve a puzzle while relaxing music is played in the background.

- TalkLife, an app that creates an online community so people can reach out to others. It helps people connect with others who are experiencing similar feelings, get support, and support others.

- Lantern, an app that allows people to connect with a personal coach if they want to talk or browse through CBT practices they can do immediately to feel better.

## The Pros and Cons of Technology

Another way technology has helped people with phobias is through the development of the internet as well as affordable personal computers and smart-phones. Texting was invented in 1992 and became widespread around the turn of the century; by 2007, Americans were receiving more texts per month than phone calls. This was a huge benefit to people with a phobia of speaking on the phone, allowing them to have more contact with their friends as well as occasionally make appointments and get information from businesses. The evolution of the internet has helped people in similar ways through the use of chat programs and message boards. Someone with a phobia of driving who might have found it hard to get to and from college classes every day can now take classes online, allowing them to earn a degree. Some companies also allow employees to work from home, which could be beneficial for someone with acrophobia whose office is on the top floor of a skyscraper. While most people with a phobia do not have problems leaving their house, the option of having what they need at home can help them keep their daily anxiety levels manageable as they work with a therapist on confronting their fears.

Another important way computers can help people with phobias is by allowing them "to establish online support groups that provide opportunities for individuals to network with others who experience similar issues,"[39] according to psychologists Virginia Smith Harvey and Janet F. Carlson. Not only is this helpful for people who have some kind of social phobia, such as speaking in front of others, it has given access to help and support to people who never had it before. This includes people who live in small towns where support services are difficult to find or get to as well as people who cannot afford to see a therapist.

Working from home can help people with certain phobias manage their anxiety levels.

Although technology has many benefits for people with phobias, it should not be seen as a substitute for treatment. Today, many people make memes that turn their poor coping mechanisms into a joke, which makes them seem normal. Additionally, while acceptance of mental health issues has increased, there are some people who have taken this idea too far. This is especially prevalent on the blogging website Tumblr, where, as one user named Gillian Andrews noted, "It became cool to define yourself by mental illness ... Like, in order to be interesting or valid, you had to have some kind of it."[40] In some cases, people have been helped by their participation on Tumblr, where they can share their stories and receive confirmation from others that they still have worth—something their mental illness might convince them is untrue.

While accepting people who have a mental illness is good, the glorification of mental illness has led many users to avoid seeking treatment. Another Tumblr user, Swedish student Hampus Leijon, felt that Tumblr romanticizes mental illness: "Just making it seem like—depression, suicide, this is cool. If you want to be part of the club, you gotta be insecure and unstable in some way. I'm not a fan."[41] Others disagree that suicide is seen as cool or a desirable course of action but agree that mental illness as a whole is frequently romanticized online. Experts say there is a fine line between people accepting themselves as unique individuals—and understanding that having a mental illness does not make them a broken or bad person—and believing that if they treat and control their mental illness, they will no longer be as interesting or special as they once were. In an article for the online magazine *Study Breaks*, which publishes content about media and culture written by college students, University of Warwick student Jen Tombs explained,

*Having a community of people struggling with the same things as you, being able to talk about your experiences without shame and knowing depression isn't your fault are all incredibly important. But if applied in the wrong way … the all-in-it-together vibe instead becomes a we-can-never-get-better one …*

*There's no secret trick to having good mental health; for many it's a constant, exhausting uphill battle. But to start that battle, the*

*conversation needs to shift beyond the mire of products and memes that it's all too easy to get stuck in online. The online landscape desperately needs to change, to foster an environment of support rather than just an atmosphere of a half-joking sort of resignation.*[42]

Left untreated, a phobia of one thing may lead to more kinds of phobias as well as to depression and thoughts of self-harm and suicide. If the person allows themselves to be convinced that avoiding their phobias instead of facing them is a normal course of action and that having a phobia makes them understand life better than someone who does not have a mental illness, they will continue to have problems in the future.

## Fearing Technology

The fear of technology, or technophobia, may seem like it must be modern. However, this fear has been around since the Industrial Revolution, when many things started to become motorized. In some cases, being concerned about new technology made sense, blurring the line between fear and phobia. For example, when electricity was first adapted for use in homes and businesses, it was fairly dangerous. Author Bill Bryson explained,

*As electricity became more freely available, many people found it unnerving to be relying for comfort on an invisible force that could swiftly and silently kill. Most electricians were hastily trained and all were necessarily inexperienced ... In 1896, [Thomas] Edison's former partner Franklin Pope electrocuted himself while working on the wiring in his own house, proving to many people's satisfaction that electricity was too dangerous even for experts. Fires due to electrical faults were not uncommon. Lightbulbs sometimes exploded, always startlingly, sometimes disastrously.*[43]

While it would have made sense for people at this time to fear electricity due to the possibility of electrocution or fires, some people developed a phobia, blaming electricity for "eyestrain, head-aches, general unhealthiness, and possibly even 'the premature exhaustion of life.' One architect was certain electric light caused freckles."[44] With the development of safety features and the training

Although this toaster is an antique today, it was a relatively new invention in 1914. Someone who refused to use it when it first came out might be labeled a technophobe today.

of skilled electricians, the dangers associated with electricity dropped dramatically. Today, anyone who refuses to have electricity in their house would likely be diagnosed with technophobia.

Most modern-day phobias do not have official clinical terms, but this does not mean they do not exist. Phobia specialist Martin Antony noted, "There is no question that some individuals are fearful of technology or of particular gadgets for various reasons."[45] However, there is "very little data in scientific literature about tech-related phobias and anxieties,"[46] according to psychologist Marla Deibler. Some phobias that did not exist in the past include nomophobia (fear of being without a phone), cyberphobia (fear of computers), and selfiephobia (fear of selfies). Some of these—in particular, selfiephobia—are not considered official phobias by experts, but as research continues, researchers may decide to add them to the next version of the *DSM*.

Phobias thrive on technology in other ways too. Today, anyone can watch a video of practically anything online. People who watch violent or disturbing scenes on YouTube or other video websites may develop phobias of things that are not at all likely to happen to them. In severe cases, this can lead to agoraphobia. For example, someone who sees a video of a terrorist attack may stop going to certain places where they believe they are likely to experience such an attack themselves. In reality, the chances of becoming a victim of terrorism are close to zero in the United States, Canada, and Europe. Each year, Americans have a higher chance of dying from cancer, a car accident, falling out of bed, being struck by lightning, playing football, or choking on food than they do of being killed in a terrorist attack.

Many people get annoyed when they realize they have left their phone at home, but some people panic. They may be afraid they will need it for an emergency or worry that they have lost it somewhere.

The media is partially responsible for the creation of certain phobias, according to phobia researcher Peter N. Stearns:

> *Americans fear levels of crime that do not exist, even when actual crime rates are falling, because of media portrayals ... They worry about child abduction or teenage gambling when both are extremely rare, again because journalists so often tell them that youth are at far greater risk than adults realize ... They make huge mistakes about the likelihood of certain feared diseases.*[47]

Although phobias have existed for thousands of years and are likely to exist for thousands more, people can take comfort in the fact that there are ways to address them. As medical and scientific knowledge continue to evolve, the ways in which phobias are identified and treated will improve as well. Working to increase understanding of phobias, both by the medical community and the general public, can also minimize the distress people feel from their phobias.

# NOTES

## Chapter One:
## Understanding Phobias

1. Quoted in "Classifying Anxiety: Understanding the Difference Between Fear and Phobia," Grace College Online, accessed on October 3, 2018. online.grace.edu/news/human-services/difference-between-fear-and-phobia/.

2. "Severity Measure for Specific Phobia—Adult," American Psychiatric Association, accessed on October 3, 2018. www.psychiatry.org/psychiatrists/practice/dsm/educational-resources/assessment-measures.

3. Quoted in Jeffrey Slonim, "The Horror," *Artforum International*, April 1994, p. 11.

4. Quoted in Slonim, "The Horror," p. 11.

5. "Tornado Alley," National Oceanic and Atmospheric Administration, accessed on October 3, 2018. www.ncdc.noaa.gov/climate-information/extreme-events/us-tornado-climatology/tornado-alley.

6. Quoted in "Severe Weather Fears Can Be Debilitating," *USA Today*, December 1996, p. 8.

7. "Everything You Should Know About Astraphobia," Healthline, accessed on October 3, 2018. www.healthline.com/health/astraphobia.

8. Lynne L. Hall, "Fighting Phobias: The Things That Go Bump in the Mind," *FDA Consumer*, March 1997, p. 12.

9. "Why We Prefer 'Social Anxiety' to 'Social Phobia,'" Social Anxiety Institute, accessed on October 12, 2018. socialanxietyinstitute.org/why-we-prefer-social-anxiety-social-phobia.

## Chapter Two:
## Risk Factors

10. Helen Saul, *Phobias: Fighting the Fear.* New York, NY: Arcade, 2004, p. 164.

11. Madeleine Brindley, "Fears and Phobias That Can Spiral Out of Control," *Western Mail*, April 9, 2007.

12. Brindley, "Fears and Phobias."

13. Quoted in Lucy Elkins, "Don't Panic (It's Only a Fish!)," *Daily Mail*, April 17, 2007.

14. Quoted in Mary Keenan and Tessa Cunningham, "Phobias: Why the Everyday World Terrifies Us," *Mirror*, April 11, 1998.

15. Susan Brown, "Fear in the Genes," *Nature*, April 8, 2008. www.nature.com/news/2008/080408/full/news.2008.743.html.

16. Kendra Cherry, "How the Availability Heuristic Affects Decision-Making," Verywell Mind, last updated September 10, 2018. www.verywellmind.com/availability-heuristic-2794824.

## Chapter Three:
## Life with Phobias

17. Susan Stevens, "Face Your Fears: Conquering Phobias Requires Marshaling Your Brain's Cognitive Power," *Daily Herald*, October 25, 2004.

18. Quoted in Alison Griswold, "Christine Blasey Ford Can Fear Flying and Still Fly," *Quartz*, September 27, 2018. qz.com/1405027/kavanaugh-hearing-christine-blasey-fords-fear-of-flying-probed/.

19. Griswold, "Christine Blasey Ford Can Fear Flying."

20. J. K. Rowling, *Harry Potter and the Chamber of Secrets*. New York, NY: Scholastic, 1999, pp. 196–197.

21. Jennifer Peepas, "My Husband Stops Talking Only When He Is Asleep and Sometimes Not Even Then," *Captain Awkward*, September 18, 2018. captainawkward.com/2018/09/18/1145-my-husband-stops-talking-only-when-he-is-asleep-and-sometimes-not-even-then/#more-45841.

22. John R. Marshall, *Social Phobia: From Shyness to Stage Fright*. New York, NY: BasicBooks, 1994, p. 152.

## Chapter Four:
## Therapy and Other Treatments

23. Gavin Andrews, "Epidemiology of Phobias: A Review," in *Phobias*, eds. Mario Maj, Hagop S. Akiskal, Juan José Lopez-Ibor, and Ahmed Okasha. Hoboken, NJ: Wiley, 2004, p. 77.

24. Marshall, *Social Phobia*, p. 30.

25. Edmund J. Bourne, *The Anxiety and Phobia Workbook*, 4th ed. Oakland, CA: New Harbinger, 2005, p. 157.

26. Alison Palkhivala, "Stressed? Take Heart ... Beta Blockers for Anxiety Can Be Effective," *University Health News*, December 29, 2016.

universityhealthnews.com/daily/stress-anxiety/
beta-blockers-for-anxiety/.

27. Mayo Clinic Staff, "Specific Phobias," Mayo Clinic, October 19, 2016. www. mayoclinic.org/diseases-conditions/ specific-phobias/diagnosis-treatment/drc-20355162.

28. Mark R. Leary and Robin M. Kowalski, "The Self-Presentation Model of Social Phobia," in *Social Phobia: Diagnosis, Assessment, and Treatment*, eds. Richard C. Heimberg, Michael R. Leibowitz, Debra A. Hope, and Franklin R. Schneier. New York, NY: Guilford, 1995, p. 104.

29. Michelle G. Crasky, Martin M. Antony, and David H. Barlow, *Mastering Your Fears and Phobias: Therapist Guide*, 2nd ed. New York, NY: Oxford University Press, 2006, p. 100.

30. Stevens, "Face Your Fears."

31. Marshall, *Social Phobia*, p. 173.

32. J. Lyman MacInnis, *The Elements of Great Public Speaking: How to Be Calm, Confident, and Compelling*. Berkeley, CA: Ten Speed Press, 2006, pp. 12–13.

33. Andrews, "Epidemiology of Phobias," p. 75.

34. Quoted in Katie Charles, "Post-Traumatic Stress Disorder Affects a Wide Range of People, Not Just Soldiers," *NY Daily News*, July 14, 2013. www.nydailynews.com/ life-style/health/ptsd-affects-people-military-article-1.1393098.

35. Chris Weller, "Most Mental Health Problems in Teens Go Untreated; Phobias, Anxiety Among the Worst," Medical Daily, November 19, 2013. www.medicaldaily.com/

most-mental-health-problems-teens-go-un-treated-phobias-anxiety-among-worst-263174.

36. Weller, "Most Mental Health Problems in Teens Go Untreated."

## Chapter Five: Looking Forward

37. Kathy Feldman, "Virtual Reality Therapy and How It Helped," Virtual Reality Medical Center, accessed on April 15, 2008. www.vrphobia.com/Feldman.htm.

38. Max M. North, Sarah M. North, and Joseph R. Coble, "Virtual Reality Therapy: An Effective Treatment for Psychological Disorders," in *Handbook of Virtual Environments: Design, Implementation, and Applications*, ed. Kay M. Stanney. Mahwah, NJ: Lawrence Erlbaum Associates, 2002, p. 1066.

39. Virginia Smith Harvey and Janet F. Carlson, "Ethical and Professional Issues with Computer-Related Technology," *School Psychology Review* 32, 2003, p. 1.

40. Quoted in Rachel Premack, "Tumblr's Depression Connection," The Ringer, October 24, 2016. www.theringer.com/2016/10/24/16041350/tumblr-communities-depression-mental-illness-anxiety-c2ca927cd305.

41. Quoted in Premack, "Tumblr's Depression Connection."

42. Jen Tombs, "Why Tumblr Might Be Hindering Your Mental Health," *Study Breaks*, August 18, 2018. studybreaks.com/thoughts/tumblr-mental-health/.

43. Bill Bryson, *At Home: A Short History of Private Life*. New York, NY: Doubleday, 2010, e-book.

44. Bryson, *At Home*, e-book.

45. Quoted in Kyli Singh, "5 Tech Phobias You Never Knew Existed," Mashable, August 2, 2014. mashable.com/2014/08/02/tech-phobias/#PbsZpGGYEsqR.

46. Singh, "5 Tech Phobias."

47. Peter N. Stearns, "Fear and Contemporary History: A Review Essay," *Journal of Social History*, vol. 40, no. 2, 2006, p. 477.

**antianxiety drug:** A medication that reduces feelings of stress, worry, or anxiety.

**antidepressant:** A medication to help with symptoms of chronic, severe sadness.

**anxiety:** Feelings of intense fear or worry about an event or situation.

**biofeedback:** A therapy method that involves performing relaxation techniques while monitoring the body's responses.

**cognitive behavioral therapy:** A method of treating phobias and other mental illnesses by changing the patient's negative thoughts.

**depression:** A deep, lasting feeling of sadness and hopelessness.

**exposure therapy:** A method of treating phobias by gradually and repeatedly exposing the patient to their trigger.

**panic:** The sudden, overpowering feeling of terror, generally marked by sweating, shortness of breath, racing heart, and a need to escape.

**specific phobia:** The strong, lasting fear of a particular object, animal, or situation.

**virtual reality therapy:** The use of artificial environments created by computers to treat phobias and other disorders.

# ORGANIZATIONS TO CONTACT

**Anxiety Disorders Association of America (ADAA)**
8701 Georgia Avenue, Suite 412
Silver Spring, MD 20910
(240) 485-1001
information@adaa.org
adaa.org
The ADAA is a national network, founded in 1979, to promote the health of people with phobias and other anxiety disorders. Its website includes tips for managing anxiety, an online support group, and a find-a-therapist tool. Always ask a parent or guardian before participating in an online forum.

**Mental Health America**
500 Montgomery Street, Suite 820
Alexandria, VA 22314
(800) 969-6642
www.mentalhealthamerica.net
Mental Health America is a nonprofit mental health organization in the United States. Its goal is to provide information about public health and help people find resources, research, and services to deal with mental problems such as anxiety and phobias.

**National Institute of Mental Health (NIMH) Office of Science Policy, Planning, and Communications**
6001 Executive Boulevard, Room 6200, MSC 9663
Bethesda, MD 20892
(866) 615-6464
nimhinfo@nih.gov
www.nimh.nih.gov
The world's largest scientific organization dedicated to mental health, NIMH has information, resources, and research about a wide variety of mental conditions, including phobias.

**National Suicide Prevention Lifeline**
(800) 273-8255
suicidepreventionlifeline.org
People who live with an untreated, severe phobia for a long time sometimes find themselves thinking of suicide, especially if their trigger is something they encounter frequently. This phone line is available at all times to connect people to a trained listener. For those who do not want to speak on the phone, the website offers a live chat option.

**University of California, Los Angeles (UCLA) Semel Institute for Neuroscience and Human Behavior's Anxiety Disorders Program**
760 Westwood Plaza
Los Angeles, CA 90095
(310) 206-5133
www.semel.ucla.edu/adc
A research facility at the University of California, Los Angeles, the Semel Institute provides one of the finest programs in the United States for the study and treatment of anxiety disorders and phobias.

## Books

Iorizzo, Carrie. *Anxiety and Phobias*. St. Catharines, Ontario: Crabtree Publishing, 2014.
This book discusses phobias and other anxiety disorders, including how to care for a loved one who is experiencing one of these issues.

Latta, Sara. *Scared Stiff: Everything You Need to Know About 50 Famous Phobias*. San Francisco, CA: Zest Books, 2013.
In addition to discussing individual phobias, this book gives information about famous people who have dealt with phobias as well as coping mechanisms people can use when they encounter their trigger.

Shannon, Jennifer. *The Anxiety Survival Guide for Teens: CBT Skills to Overcome Fear, Worry & Panic*. Oakland, CA: Instant Help Books, 2015.
Shannon helps teens identify which type of anxiety disorder they suffer from and, through skills associated with cognitive behavioral therapy, overcome their fears to become more confident.

Umbach, Andrea. *Conquer Your Fears and Phobias for Teens: How to Build Courage and Stop Fear from Holding You Back*. Oakland, CA: New Harbinger Publications, 2015.
This workbook uses CBT skills to help teens overcome their phobias. This is a good introductory resource for people who are not yet ready to see a therapist or who are unable to afford one.

# Websites

### Depression Forums
*www.depressionforums.org/forums/*
Anxiety and depression frequently go hand in hand, as the stress of dealing with an anxiety disorder such as a phobia can cause depression or make it worse. This website allows people with depression to discuss their issues with other people who understand what they are going through. Always ask a parent or guardian before participating in an online forum.

### Institute of Living
*instituteofliving.org*
This website, which is a division of Hartford Hospital in Connecticut, includes information about anxiety disorders such as phobias. Visitors to the website can take a short quiz to see if they have the symptoms of a phobia. This is not intended to diagnose a person, only to help them decide whether to seek further help from a professional.

### National Alliance on Mental Illness (NAMI)
*www.nami.org*
NAMI is a national nonprofit outreach, educational, and advocacy organization dedicated to improving the lives of people with mental illnesses and their families.

### The Tribe Wellness Community
*support.therapytribe.com/anxiety-support-group/*
This online support group for anxiety disorders allows people to connect with others who are suffering from the same thing. A link is provided to help people find therapists near them.

## A

## B

## C

# PICTURE CREDITS

# ABOUT THE AUTHOR

**Maeve Losito** was born and raised in Buffalo, New York, along with her siblings. She is an aspiring novelist who has participated in National Novel Writing Month and self-published a book before graduating high school to begin her journey into the publication field. She attended Niagara University and received a bachelor's degree in English with a concentration in writing studies. She plans to continue her education to obtain a master's degree in fiction, as well as gain further experiences to better her skills as a writer.